Christian Faith Perspectives in Leadership and Business

Series Editors
Kathleen Patterson
School of Global Leadership and Entrepre
Regent University
Virginia Beach, VA, USA

Doris Gomez
Regent University
Virginia Beach, VA, USA

Bruce E. Winston
Regent University
Virginia Beach, VA, USA

Gary Oster
Regent University
Virginia Beach, VA, USA

This book series is designed to integrate Christian faith-based perspectives into the field of leadership and business, widening its influence by taking a deeper look at its foundational roots. It is led by a team of experts from Regent University, recognized by the Coalition of Christian Colleges and Universities as the leader in servant leadership research and the first Christian University to integrate innovation, design thinking, and entrepreneurship courses in its Masters and Doctoral programs. Stemming from Regent's hallmark values of innovation and Christian faith-based perspectives, the series aims to put forth top-notch scholarship from current faculty, students, and alumni of Regent's School of Business & Leadership, allowing for both scholarly and practical aspects to be addressed while providing robust content and relevant material to readers. Each volume in the series will contribute to filling the void of a scholarly Christian-faith perspective on key aspects of organizational leadership and business such as Business and Innovation, Biblical Perspectives in Business and Leadership, and Servant Leadership. The series takes a unique approach to such broad-based and well-trodden disciplines as leadership, business, innovation, and entrepreneurship, positioning itself as a much-needed resource for students, academics, and leaders rooted in Christian-faith traditions.

More information about this series at
http://www.palgrave.com/gp/series/15425

Maurice A. Buford

Bold Followership

A Biblical Cure for Organizational Toxicity

Maurice A. Buford
Regent University
Virginia Beach, USA

That the views in this book are the opinion of the author alone and do not necessarily reflect the views of the Department of Defense.

Christian Faith Perspectives in Leadership and Business
ISBN 978-3-319-74529-9   ISBN 978-3-319-74530-5   (eBook)
https://doi.org/10.1007/978-3-319-74530-5

Library of Congress Control Number: 2018935391

© The Editor(s) (if applicable) and The Author(s) 2018
This work is subject to copyright. All rights are solely and exclusively licensed by the Publisher, whether the whole or part of the material is concerned, specifically the rights of translation, reprinting, reuse of illustrations, recitation, broadcasting, reproduction on microfilms or in any other physical way, and transmission or information storage and retrieval, electronic adaptation, computer software, or by similar or dissimilar methodology now known or hereafter developed.
The use of general descriptive names, registered names, trademarks, service marks, etc. in this publication does not imply, even in the absence of a specific statement, that such names are exempt from the relevant protective laws and regulations and therefore free for general use.
The publisher, the authors, and the editors are safe to assume that the advice and information in this book are believed to be true and accurate at the date of publication. Neither the publisher nor the authors or the editors give a warranty, express or implied, with respect to the material contained herein or for any errors or omissions that may have been made. The publisher remains neutral with regard to jurisdictional claims in published maps and institutional affiliations.

Cover illustration: Peter Fakler / Alamy Stock Photo

Printed on acid-free paper

This Palgrave Macmillan imprint is published by the registered company Springer International Publishing AG part of Springer Nature.
The registered company address is: Gewerbestrasse 11, 6330 Cham, Switzerland

ACKNOWLEDGMENTS

Scripture taken from the New King James Version® (NKJV). Copyright © 1982 by Thomas Nelson. Used by permission. All rights reserved.

CONTENTS

1	A King in Narcissistic Clothes	1
2	Decoding the Silence	19
3	You Have the Right to Remain Silent. Or Do You?	43
4	Faithful Are the Wounds of a Friend	59
5	A Prescription for Organizational Dis-eases	73
6	Walking Away to Win the Day	91
7	If It Is to Be, It Is Left Up to We: The People, by People, and for the People	107
8	Measuring Your Organization's Boardroom Language	119
9	The Anatomy of Bold Followership	147
	Bibliography	161
	Index	167

LIST OF FIGURES

Fig. 1.1	The leadership little fox trap	11
Fig. 1.2	Spiritual intuition model	14
Fig. 2.1	King David's royal court	20
Fig. 2.2	Good apples, bad barrels, and ugly barrel makers, based on Zimbardo's (2008) "Psychology of Evil" Ted Talk	22
Fig. 2.3	The seven factors of a spiritual organization	25
Fig. 3.1	Boardroom boldness language model—quadrant I	44
Fig. 3.2	The ethical pause model	46
Fig. 3.3	The spectrum of "shut up" boardroom language	58
Fig. 4.1	Boardroom boldness language model—quadrant II	61
Fig. 4.2	The aspects of speaking in	69
Fig. 4.3	The spectrum of "speak in" boardroom language	71
Fig. 5.1	Boardroom boldness language model—quadrant III	81
Fig. 5.2	Clausewitz's trinity	81
Fig. 5.3	The spectrum of "speak in" boardroom language	89
Fig. 6.1	Boardroom boldness language model—quadrant IV	97
Fig. 6.2	The spectrum of the "step-down" boardroom language	104
Fig. 7.1	Boardroom boldness language model—quadrant V	108
Fig. 7.2	The step it up model	113
Fig. 7.3	The reflective leadership model	115
Fig. 7.4	The spectrum of the "step it up" boardroom language	116

LIST OF TABLES

Table 1.1	The little foxes of leadership	4
Table 2.1	The biblical source of boldness	34
Table 3.1	A tale of two complying organizations	52
Table 8.1	Boardroom boldness items	121
Table 8.2	Age	124
Table 8.3	Gender	124
Table 8.4	Income	125
Table 8.5	Region	128
Table 8.6	Shut-up correlation matrix	129
Table 8.7	Regenerated shut-up pattern matrix	131
Table 8.8	Shut-up and comply scale	131
Table 8.9	Shut-up and sabotage scale	132
Table 8.10	Speak-in correlation matrix	133
Table 8.11	Speak-in pattern matrix	134
Table 8.12	Speak-in with a parable scale	135
Table 8.13	Speak-in on principles	135
Table 8.14	Speak-out correlation matrix	136
Table 8.15	Speak-out pattern matrix	137
Table 8.16	Speak-out nonviolently scale	138
Table 8.17	Speak-out negatively scale	138
Table 8.18	Step-down correlation matrix	140
Table 8.19	Step-down pattern matrix	141
Table 8.20	Step-down by resigning scale	141
Table 8.21	Step-down by resisting scale	141
Table 8.22	Step-it-up correlation matrix	142
Table 8.23	Step-it-up pattern matrix	143
Table 8.24	Shut-up and comply scale	144

xii LIST OF TABLES

Table 8.25	Shut-up and sabotage scale	144
Table 8.26	Speak-in with a parable scale	145
Table 8.27	Speak-in on principles scale	145
Table 8.28	Speak-out negatively scale	145
Table 8.29	Speak-out nonviolently scale	146
Table 8.30	Step-down by resisting scale	146
Table 8.31	Step-down by resigning scale	146
Table 9.1	The biblical traits of a bold follower	153

INTRODUCTION

An analysis of *Global Trends 2030* may suggest that organizational perplexities, moral ambiguities, and leadership vacuums will challenge the twenty-first century workforce.[1] Such a test will seemingly call into question traditional constructs affiliated with power, trust, and nationalist ideologies. How well organizations brace, respond, and proactively navigate the uncharted terrain of uncertainty could very well be the ultimate difference maker. The critical key to thriving in the ensuing shifting sands of change will not come from without but rather from within. Stated differently, though technologies and information affiliated with the workforce may continue to transform; the spirit of we the people remains the same. That spirit that motivates the powerless to be strong is currently in operation behind the cubicle dividers across the workforce. That spirit that called warriors to lay down their lives for the liberties of a nation is still active in the ranks of the armed forces. That spirit that enabled truth-tellers to articulate uncomfortable realities to those in command is still advising, but now such voices seem to need a better model to equip them to stand more effectively.

Therefore the driving question of this book becomes, "Can the sacred text provide a template to help organizations build a wise and moral boardroom boldness to help mitigate executive ethical mishaps?" To resolve this inquiry, an analysis is conducted in Chap. 1 of King David's executive decision to carry out a census of Israel, as outlined in 2 Samuel 24 and 1 Chronicles 21. This exegetical deliberation first explores the perplexities followers might experience when their anointed leaders suddenly make a toxic choice. In Chap. 2 this provocative conversation then introduces the reader to a boardroom boldness language model (BBLM) that appears to capture the spectrum of concerned voices as they respectfully endeavor to lead upward. To further operationalize the BBLM, Joab is introduced to the reader. Chapter 3 attempts to illuminate a specific course of action while highlighting other options within quadrant I of the BBLM. In Chap. 4 quadrant II of the BBLM is outlined by presenting a methodology abstracted from Gad, the seer, which is predicated upon the level of trust a follower can have in a toxically blinded leader.

Chapter 5 examines quadrant III of the BBLM while exploring the nuances of *organizational dis-eases*. This discourse sets the stage for wrestling with the difficulties of the BBLM's final quadrant. Chapter 6 walks the reader through several scenarios that may require a leader to step down for the health of the organization. After scrutinizing the various elements of the BBLM, a critical lens is then applied in Chap. 7 to the question, "Are there a particular set of attributes that can help messengers of truth to communicate better?" Chapter 8 should help followers to discern the motives of their style of followership and to develop a scale to measure organizational health. Finally, the reader is challenged with a series of introspective questions, and a discussion outlined on how to lead after the storm of toxicity has subsided, and the research question of this book is given a plausible explanation

NOTE

1. Kojm, Christopher. 2012. *Global Trends 2030: Alternative Worlds.* December. Accessed March 6, 2017. https://worldview.unc.edu/files/2013/10/Global-Trends-2030-Executive-Summary

CHAPTER 1

A King in Narcissistic Clothes

A King in Narcissistic Clothes

What happens when an adversary stands up against a nation, an organization, community or even a home? 1 Chronicles 21:1–2 suggests that the head of an entity may very well become the inadvertent instrument of corporate demise. In the case of King David, his Achille's heel may have always been present, but the friction and temptation of the moment introduced it to the world. Namely, the possible blind spot that temporarily transformed an anointed and charismatic warrior into a toxic decision maker was arrogance. Arrogance, according to Merriam-Webster, can be described as exaggerating or disposed to exaggerate one's worth or importance, often in an overbearing manner. Such a manner, arguably, was noticed by his family long before David became a household name. 1 Samuel 17:28–29 indicates that

> Now Eliab his oldest brother heard when he spoke to the men; and Eliab's anger was aroused against David, and he said, "Why did you come down here? And with whom have you left those few sheep in the wilderness? I know your pride and the insolence of your heart, for you have come down to see the battle."[29] And David said, "What have I done now? *Is there* not a cause?"

This text records Eliab's reaction without understanding that David was being sent by his father to serve them and that the sheep were properly cared for by another shepherd. Additionally, this passage seems to illuminate

© The Author(s) 2018
M. A. Buford, *Bold Followership*, Christian Faith Perspectives in Leadership and Business, https://doi.org/10.1007/978-3-319-74530-5_1

1

a deeply held perception that has not received much attention in biblical leadership dialog. Namely, the older brother knew "the pride and the insolence" of his younger brother David. Moreover, when this sibling charge was offered, what is interesting to note is David's reaction. He did not deny the accusation but confirmed it with his questions, *What have I done now? Is there not a cause?* Perhaps an inference of David's response is that other incidents could have resonated and were not recorded, but this was not necessarily one of them?

Although Scripture indicates that Satan stood up against Israel and that David was moved to number the nation, it does not exactly spell out the nature of the transgression. This theological ambiguity has sparked an array of theories, but the logic of Matthew Henry resonates when he asserted that, "Numbering the people, one would think, was no bad thing. Why should not the shepherd know the number of his flock? But God sees not as man sees. It is plain it was wrong in David to do it, and a great provocation to God, because he did it in the pride of his heart; and there is no sin that has in it more of contradiction and therefore more of offense to God than pride."[1]

In retrospect, one can see how David's vice could have remained dormant until provoked at this point in his career. To better understand, a cursory review of the king's calling is delineated. First, it should be noted that David was not the preferred son of Jesse when the Prophet came to anoint the next king. In fact, this marginalized shepherd boy had to be asked for by Samuel when his family overlooked him (1 Sam 16:11–12). Next, David's rise to prominence began when he defeated the giant from Philistine, he took on a key leadership position in the royal ranks and his popularity expanded as he ran from a jealous King Saul who vowed to end David's life. When fate took a turn, and King Saul fell on his sword, David assumed the throne. This defining moment signaled to the world that finally Israel had found a champion, a warrior and king like none other.

As king, David united Israel and achieved numerous accomplishments through the hand of God. Debatably, such triumphs set the conditions during a time when kings went to war, for David to make the decision to remain behind (2 Sam 11). This costly decision would prove to be painful and long lasting because an adulterous affair ensued, an innocent husband was murdered, and a sword forever pierced the household of David. This

---

[1] Henry, M. (1994). *Matthew Henry's commentary on the whole Bible: complete and unabridged in one volume* (p. 574). Peabody: Hendrickson.

A KING IN NARCISSISTIC CLOTHES 3

sword provoked his children to stir up strife in the kingdom and propelled his most beloved son, Absalom, to challenge him for the throne. After a season of fleeing and fighting, the coup was surpressed, and yet another of David's loved ones had passed away, but he had regained the kingdom. It is at this point of renewed power, when there are emotions of triumph and the temptation to take a metaphorical victory lap, that this book cautions leaders to take heed. For it is during such moments that dormant unprocessed matters of the heart may emerge and undermine one's ability to be a moral influence. In the case of David, it was the pride and the insolence of his heart as described by his oldest brother Eliab that would set the conditions for a humble king to be transformed temporarily into a narcissist.

CATCHING THE LITTLE FOXES

This notion of overlooked issues, or the inability to connect the proverbial dots of dormant personality flaws, warrants consideration. To help explore this phenomenon the wisdom of Solomon, David's son and heir to the throne, is invoked. Namely, Bathsheba's son admonishes influencers in Solomon 2:15 to, "Catch us the foxes, the little foxes that spoil vines, for our vines have tender grapes." Although this text has an array of scholarly interpretations, this book utilizes Jamieson, Fausset and Brown's (1997) understanding of foxes. Jamieson et al. suggest that foxes are a:

> generic term, including jackals. They eat only grapes, not the vine flowers; but they need to be driven out *in time* before the grape is ripe. She had failed in watchfulness before (So 1:6); now when converted, she is the more jealous of *subtle* sins (Ps 139:23). In spiritual winter certain evils are frozen up, as well as good; in the spring of revivals these start up unperceived, crafty, false teachers, spiritual pride, uncharitableness, &c. (Ps 19:12; Mt 13:26; Lu 8:14; 2 Ti 2:17; Heb 12:15). "Little" sins are parents of the greatest (Ec 10:1; 1 Co 5:6).[2]

If, in fact, little foxes are parents of the greatest, then the question becomes, "Who specifically are these guardians, what are their characteristics and how should they be handled?" To offer a plausible biblical explanation to such an inquiry, consider 1 John 2:16 "For all that *is* in the world—the lust of the flesh, the lust of the eyes, and the pride of life—is

[2] Jamieson, R., Fausset, A. R., & Brown, D. (1997). *Commentary Critical and Explanatory on the Whole Bible* (Vol. 1, p. 419). Oak Harbor, WA: Logos Research Systems, Inc.

not of the Father but is of the world." This text essentially introduces the reader to the three categories of "parents," or foxes, that a leader will face.

THE LITTLE FOX OF THE EYES

As depicted in Table 1.1, the first fox that a leader should monitor is lust of the eyes, when an influencer may have the impulse to pursue the stimulations of what they see. Although the longings associated with the eyes are broad and limitless, perhaps the central vice that captivates most imaginations revolves around sexual relations outside of marriage. A famous biblical example, outlined in Judges 16:1–5, illuminates this point.

> Now Samson went to Gaza and saw a harlot there, and went in to her.[2] When the Gazites *were told*, "Samson has come here!" they surrounded *the place* and lay in wait for him all night at the gate of the city. They were quiet all night, saying, "In the morning, when it is daylight, we will kill him."[3] And Samson lay *low* till midnight; then he arose at midnight, took hold of the doors of the gate of the city and the two gateposts, pulled them up, bar and all, put *them* on his shoulders, and carried them to the top of the hill that faces Hebron.[4] Afterward it happened that he loved a woman in the Valley of Sorek, whose name *was* Delilah.[5] And the lords of the Philistines came up to her and said to her, "Entice him, and find out where his great strength *lies*, and by what *means* we may overpower him, that we may bind him to afflict him; and every one of us will give you eleven hundred *pieces* of silver."

Table 1.1 The little foxes of leadership

Little foxes	Trait	Biblical example	Case study
Lust of the eyes	Longings stimulated by what one sees. An example of this can include sexual relations outside of marriage	Samson's lust for Delilah as recorded in Judges 16 was costly	Why powerful people cheat
Lust of the flesh	The illicit cravings of the flesh. An example of this is the desire to become rich by unethical means	Judas' craving for money grew to be the fox that would betray Christ (Matt 26:14–26)	Bernard Madoff
Pride of life	The sense of arrogance that comes as a byproduct of possessions and power affiliated with this world	Nebuchadnezzar's pride made him insane as he observed the "trophy" of "his" kingdom (Dan 4:30)	Adolf Hitler

In this text, we find the strongest man that walked the planet being lured by what he saw. Namely, while on a business trip to Gaza (a city of the Philistines located in the extreme southwest of Palestine close to the Mediterranean[3]) the beauty of a woman of the night arrested his attention. This intense lust of the eyes became so strong that Samson made a decision to overlook the wisdom of Proverbs 6:26, "for by means of a harlot a man is reduced to a piece of bread," and "went into her." If it were not for the mercy and strength of the Lord in his life, this would have been a fatal move. Why? Because the Gazites' intent was to exploit this flaw by staging an ambush. However, Samson was able to outmaneuver the opposition by ripping up the entire gate structure and carrying it to a hill 38 miles away.[4] Although Samson had successfully removed himself from that particular battle, his inward war with the lust of the eyes was ongoing and on the verge of a final showdown.

Seemingly, Samson's fox of the lust of the eyes had grown to its full capacity when he had fallen so quickly for a woman in the Valley of Sorek whose name was Delilah. According to Wiersbe (1994, p. 121)

> scholars disagree on the meaning of Delilah's name. Some think it means "devotee," suggesting that she may have been a temple prostitute. However, Delilah is not called a prostitute as is the woman in Gaza, although that is probably what she was. For that matter, Delilah is not even identified as a Philistine. However, from her dealings with the Philistine leaders, she appears to be one. Other students believe that the basis for her name is the Hebrew word *dalal*, which means "to weaken, to impoverish." Whether or not this is the correct derivation, she certainly weakened and impoverished Samson![5]

How specifically did Delilah enfeeble Samson? She nourished Samson's uncaught fox with the food of seduction, validation, manipulation, and consternation. The result was that the vines of Samson's life were spoiled.

But does this construct apply to leaders in today's context? Sheri Meyers, while analyzing a litany of high-profile cases of infidelity, postulates

---

[3] Strong, J. (1995). *Enhanced Strong's Lexicon*. Woodside Bible Fellowship.

[4] Willmington, H. L. (1997). *Willmington's Bible handbook* (p. 130). Wheaton, IL: Tyndale House Publishers.

[5] Wiersbe, W. W. (1994). *Be available* (p. 121). Wheaton, IL: Victor Books.

that it does. The author of *Chatting or Cheating: How to detect infidelity, rebuild love and affair-proof your relationship* explains that often these influencers are Alphas. This reality often equates to higher levels of testosterone, dopamine, and risk taking. Such a drive is often what propels them to the top. Unfortunately, this same laser focus on their career can be a liability when it blurs self-care. It is this disregard for catching the little fox of the eyes earlier in their life that results in a later fall from professional grace.

THE LITTLE FOX OF THE FLESH

The second fox that deserves attention is the illicit cravings of the flesh. In a similar vein as lust of the eyes, this vice can have broad implications but the one area that fascinates the imagination of the masses is that of greed. This allure to obtain fame, power, or riches by an unethical methodology has undermined a host of leaders. A biblical case can be found in the life of Judas, traces of his lust of the flesh can be found in John 12:1–6:

> Then, six days before the Passover, Jesus came to Bethany, where Lazarus was who had been dead, whom He had raised from the dead.[2] There they made Him a supper; and Martha served, but Lazarus was one of those who sat at the table with Him.[3] Then Mary took a pound of very costly oil of spikenard, anointed the feet of Jesus, and wiped His feet with her hair. And the house was filled with the fragrance of the oil.[4] But one of His disciples, Judas Iscariot, Simon's *son*, who would betray Him, said,[5] "Why was this fragrant oil not sold for three hundred denarii and given to the poor?"[6] This he said, not that he cared for the poor, but because he was a thief, and had the money box; and he used to take what was put in it.

This passage highlights Judas' characteristics. First, he had no real regard for the poor, which is interesting because one of the pillars of the mission of Jesus is to proclaim the good news to the poor and to feed them (Luke 4:18; Matt 25:35). Second, he was viewed and known as a thief, a perception that was formulated over the course of at least three years. During this time, as he walked with Jesus, he seemingly lobbied his way into the position of Treasurer to the Christ. While in this role, Judas methodically "cooked the books" to cover up his lust of the flesh. What is interesting to note at this point is that the Savior had actionable knowledge of this fact because He is sovereign. If this is true, the questions become "Why didn't

God intervene?" and "Why not relieve Judas of this responsibility?" Perhaps God was providing him with the space of mercy to catch that little fox before it is too late, as He does for us.

Judas, regrettably, failed to maximize the space of mercy to confront his lust of the flesh. Matthew 26:14–16 confirms this assertion by indicating: "Then one of the twelve, called Judas Iscariot, went to the chief priests[15] and said, 'What are you willing to give me if I deliver Him [Jesus] to you?' And they counted out to him 30 pieces of silver.[16] So from that time he sought opportunity to betray Him." Stated slightly differently, Judas' little fox was now fully grown and was dying to feast on a ripe vineyard. Tragically, the occasion that he sought was to hand over Jesus to the authorities. When the opportune moment presented itself, Judas' lust of the flesh seemingly moved beyond the level of thief to that of betrayer. This transformation and point of no return was literally sealed with a kiss as Jesus called him a friend during the very act of disloyalty (Matt. 26:49–50). Plainly put, this lust of the flesh set the conditions for the crucifixion of Christ as well as the self-destructive act of Judas.

A modern example of the lust of the flesh is debatably the case of Bernie Madoff. This contemporary personality made history by creating the largest Ponzi scheme in the world. Such a deceitful endeavor resulted in the defrauding of 68.4 billion dollars from the funds of investors. This bold action has caused millions to ponder why as they endeavored to reconcile this unthinkable act. A plausible explanation, however, may have been in plain sight for years before Bernie Madoff's name became a synonym for greed. Jerry Oppenheimer, in an article *The Making of Madoff*, notes:

> Bernie also seems to have absorbed his parents' loose business ethics, which became apparent in his first entrepreneurial venture during high school and college: installing lawn-sprinkler systems in the yards of Long Island's new tract housing. Aware that his potential customers were young couples, including desperate housewives left alone in the suburbs all day, he hired two handsome fellow students to do the installations. According to one of them, Bernie was a good salesman, but he worked fast, and he worked dirty. "He never got the required building or work permits," says Gordon Ondis, and Bernie "was not a whiz when it came to the technical aspects of his business." Years later, Bernie was still being accosted in public by dissatisfied sprinkler-system customers.[6]

[6] Oppenheimer, Jerry. 2009. "The Daily Beast." *The Making of Madoff.* August 1. Accessed July 9, 2017. http://www.thedailybeast.com/the-making-of-madoff

8 M. A. BUFORD

This early display of Madoff's lust of the flesh had not yet reached full maturity, this account of the lawn-sprinkler system hustle is evidence that this vice was already lurking before Madoff became infamous. In a sense, he was a business accident waiting to happen on a national scale. This mishap could have been mitigated, and thousands of investors would still have their nest eggs, if this metaphorical fox had been caught when it was small.

THE FOX CALLED THE PRIDE OF LIFE

The third fox that leaders need to monitor is the pride of life. This sense of arrogance, which comes as a byproduct of possessions and power, is perhaps the deadliest of them all. A biblical case of this vice in operation can be found in Daniel 4:28–32:

> All *this* came upon King Nebuchadnezzar.[29] At the end of the twelve months he was walking about the royal palace of Babylon.[30] The king spoke, saying, "Is not this great Babylon, that I have built for a royal dwelling by my mighty power and for the honor of my majesty?"[31] While the word *was still* in the king's mouth, a voice fell from heaven: "King Nebuchadnezzar, to you it is spoken: the kingdom has departed from you![32] And they shall drive you from men, and your dwelling *shall be* with the beasts of the field. They shall make you eat grass like oxen; and seven times shall pass over you, until you know that the Most High rules in the kingdom of men, and gives it to whomever He chooses."

This passage reveals the most powerful man on the planet gloating as he observes the wealth, splendor, and might he can credit to his hands. Nebuchadnezzar, however, would soon discover the truth and wisdom in Proverbs 16:18 and 29:23, "Pride goes before destruction and a haughty spirit before a fall… A man's pride will bring him low…" In this biblical scenario, the king's haughty spirit resulted in the loss of his sound mind and his being debased to the field of the beasts. Another way to describe this conceited tendency is clinically. According to Sandhya Pruthi narcissism is a personality disorder

> in which people have traits that cause them to feel and behave in socially distressing ways, limiting their ability to function in relationships and other areas of their life, such as work or school… They often monopolize conversations, belittle or look down on people they perceive as inferior. Moreover,

they may feel a sense of entitlement—and when they do not receive special treatment, this personality type may become impatient or angry.[7]

Pruthi (1998) additionally outlines the DSM-5 criteria of a narcissistic personality by suggesting that such people are accustomed to:

- Having an exaggerated sense of self-importance
- Expecting to be recognized as superior even without achievements that warrant it
- Exaggerating your achievements and talents
- Being preoccupied with fantasies about success, power, brilliance, beauty or the perfect mate
- Believing that you are superior and can only be understood by or associate with equally special people
- Requiring constant admiration
- Having a sense of entitlement
- Expecting special favors and unquestioning compliance with your expectations
- Taking advantage of others to get what you want
- Having an inability or unwillingness to recognize the needs and feelings of others
- Being envious of others and believing others envy you
- Behaving in an arrogant or haughty manner[8]

The above criteria can easily be identified in the early life of Adolf Hitler. In *Adolf Hitler: A Study in Tyranny*, the author illuminates the formative years of one of the evilest personalities of our time by asserting that Hitler in his early years, "showed traits that characterized his later life: inability to establish ordinary human relationships; intolerance and hatred both of the established bourgeois world and of non-German peoples, especially the Jews; a tendency to passionate, denunciatory outbursts; and a readiness to live in a world of fantasy to escape from his poverty and failure."[9]

[7] Pruthi, Sandhya. 1998. "Narcissistic personality disorder." *Mayo Clinic.* Accessed August 5, 2017. http://www.mayoclinic.org/diseases-conditions/narcissistic-personality-disorder/basics/symptoms/con-20025568

[8] Pruthi, Sandhya. 1998. "Narcissistic personality disorder." *Mayo Clinic.* Accessed August 5, 2017. http://www.mayoclinic.org/diseases-conditions/narcissistic-personality-disorder/basics/symptoms/con-20025568

[9] Holocaust Teacher Resource Center. 2017. "Adolf Hitler: A Study in Tyranny." Accessed August 5, 2017. http://www.holocaust-trc.org/the-holocaust-education-program-resource-guide/a-study-in-tyranny/

Regrettably, history suggests that each of the DSM-5 traits were present in Hitler's life and that millions of innocent Jewish lives were prematurely ended due to this out of control vice and his delusional outlook on life.

The Little Leadership Fox Trap

As illustrated by the previous biblical and contemporary cases, the little foxes of leadership can have a devastating effect on both influencer and organization. McKinley Johnson, author of *The Theory of Leadership*, rightfully captures this point as he reflects on the Song of Solomon 2:15. Johnson states that

> the lesson to be gleaned here is key: it is better to deal with character flaws in their infancy than in their maturity. There seems to be a three-strike rule in play when it comes to managing moral issues. The first wake-up call is usually subtle. If you are not careful, you can miss it. The second wake-up call is an attention-getter. Typically, it is a clear message to the recipient. The third and final notice is when the person is sitting on the sidelines with their head between their hands, wondering what just happened.[10]

If Johnson is indeed correct that it is better to deal with character flaws in their infancy than in their maturity, the question becomes, "How?" How specifically could the likes of Samson, Judas, Nebuchadnezzar, and by extension us, privately confront such little leadership foxes (LLF) before they antagonize us publicly?

Logos Therapy

As displayed in Fig. 1.1, there are six biblical elements involved in catching a fox in its infancy. The first stage can be referred to as Logos therapy. John 1:1 reminds the reader that, "In the beginning was the Word, and the Word was with God, and the Word was God." In Greek the term Word is Logos, λόγος. In this verse God and Logos are revealed by the Holy Bible as one. To this end, Logos therapy can be defined as the saturation of God's Word into the heart of a leader. Psalms 119:9–11 best demonstrates the power of this procedure by asking, "How can a young

---

[10]Johnson, McKinley. 2016. *The Theory of Leadership*. Lake Mary: Creation House. p. 99

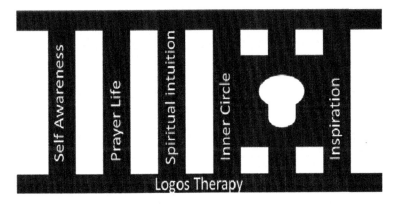

Fig. 1.1 The leadership little fox trap

man cleanse his way? By taking heed according to Your word. With my whole heart, I have sought You; Oh let me not wander from Your commandments! Your word I have hidden in my heart, That I might not sin against You." These verses illuminate the relationship between hiding the Logos deep within our heart, and pushing back on those sins that can easily overtake one.

SELF-AWARENESS

One of the principle outcomes of Logos therapy is a keener awareness of our true selves. This second component of the LLF trap can be gleaned from Hebrews 4:12–13. "For the word of God *is* living and powerful, and sharper than any two-edged sword, piercing even to the division of soul and spirit, and of joints and marrow, and is a discerner of the thoughts and intents of the heart.[13] And there is no creature hidden from His sight, but all things *are* naked and open to the eyes of Him to whom we *must give* account." As a leader spends quality time meditating on the Logos, God uses the Word to unearth the motives of the heart that often go unnoticed by the world. This discernment of the thoughts and intents of our heart will graciously reveal the type of fox (i.e., lust of the eyes, lust of the flesh, or the pride of life) that is trying to spoil the vineyard of our potential.

The self-awareness that results from hiding the Logos in our hearts will undoubtedly generate a degree of tension. Such a friction point may be the result of unreconciled self-perspectives. In other words, a leader may view themselves as a humble and selfless personality, but such a worldview may be challenged when Logos therapy reveals otherwise. To this end, the third element of the LLF trap is prayer. Biblical prayer can be defined as humanity exercising dominion on the earth (through the grace of Jesus Christ) by giving God the freedom to intervene in earth's affairs through divine petitions.[11] The following template for prayer can help a leader successfully resolve internal friction points, receive the required mercy, and an unmerited favor to persevere. Luke 11:1–4 states,

> Now it came to pass, as He was praying in a certain place, when He ceased, *that* one of His disciples said to Him, "Lord, teach us to pray, as John also taught his disciples."[2] So He said to them, "When you pray, say: Our Father in heaven, Hallowed be Your name. Your kingdom come. Your will be done On earth as *it is* in heaven.[3] Give us day by day our daily bread.[4] And forgive us our sins, For we also forgive everyone who is indebted to us. And do not lead us into temptation, But deliver us from the evil one."

PRAYING FOR THE PREY

As the disciples watched Jesus engage in fervent prayer, they seemingly made the connection between Jesus' inner life (i.e., the ability to overcome temptations) and public miracles, and concluded that prayer was the source of His power. So the disciples requested a tutorial on how to exercise dominion on the earth by giving God the freedom to intervene in earth's affairs through divine petitions. Jesus' model of prayer had seven distinct parts:

- Acknowledgment
- Yielding to God's will
- Dependence on God not things for provision
- Requesting forgiveness
- Forgiving others
- Following God's leadership
- Deliverance

[11] Munroe, Myles. 2002. *Understanding the Purpose and Power of Prayer.* New Kensington, PA: Whitaker House. p. 29

In light of the above elements, the following "fox catching" prayer can be offered by a leader to the Lord to help overcome.

> Gracious God, I acknowledge that you are supreme, holy, majestic and very concerned about the affairs of this universe. Because of your love, I understand by faith that you know the plans that you have for my life, plans to prosper and not to harm me, plans to give me hope and a future. So, God give me the strength to submit to your perfect will and not my selfish desires. I understand that the source of my strength is not by the might of things nor the power of people but that I am desperately dependent on you. Forgive me for my arrogant belief that I can lead without your guidance and that things are all about me. Because I understand that I am in frantic need of forgiveness, soften my heart to graciously forgive those that have offended me. Now God, as you make the path before me plain, render ineffective those little foxes that I have not had the courage nor insight to confront and I will follow hard after you with all my mind, body, and soul. In Jesus' name I pray. Amen.

Spiritual Intuition

Such a prayer, sincerely uttered in faith, will set the environment to be led by the Holy Spirit. The third person of the Trinity, who proceeds from the Father, is our comforter or helper (*Parakeletos* from para, "beside," and kaleo, "to call"). Hence, the Holy Spirit is an intercessor, comforter, helper, advocate, and counselor called to one's side. Jesus discussed the importance of the *Parakeletos* with His disciples in John 16:12–14:

> I still have many things to say to you, but you cannot bear *them* now.[13] However, when He, the Spirit of truth, has come, He will guide you into all truth; for He will not speak on His own *authority,* but whatever He hears He will speak; and He will tell you things to come.[14] He will glorify Me, for He will take of what is Mine and declare *it* to you.[15] All things that the Father has are Mine. Therefore, I said that He will take of Mine and declare *it* to you.

In a similar vein, Galatians 5:16–17 admonishes leaders to "Walk in the Spirit, and you shall not fulfill the lust of the flesh.[17] For the flesh lusts against the Spirit, and the Spirit against the flesh; and these are contrary to one another, so that you do not do the things that you wish." See Fig. 1.2.

Fig. 1.2 Spiritual intuition model

What does it mean to walk in the Spirit, to make sound godly choices, and overcome small foxes? Essentially, walking in the Spirit is a leader's ability to be sensitive to the still small voice of God (see 1 Kgs 19:11–13) within their gut, to arrive at a decision point, or to rightly discern a situation. As depicted in Fig. 1.1, the *Parakeletos*, as represented by the circular line (although the Spirit is as unpredictable as the wind, Jn 3:8), will often escort a leader to a wicked problem. Camillus (2008) suggests that a wicked problem has innumerable causes, is tough to describe, and does not appear to have a right answer.[12] It is in this place of darkness, affiliated with ambiguity, that the *Parakeletos'* light shines best.

As an influencer grapples with an issue, the *Parakeletos* will process that situation through the lens of the Logos. More specifically, the Spirit will quickly endeavor to unearth a course of action that aligns with the principles of the Word. This is, debatably, an essential element of the spiritual intuition model since the Spirit will never contradict or violate the precepts of the Logos. To this end, it is a leadership imperative to engage frequently in Logos therapy. The more that a leader abides in the Word, the quicker the wickedness of the problem set will be mitigated (Jn 15:4–8). After the Holy Spirit processes the dilemma through the guide of the Logos, the glorify gage is employed. That is, the *Parakeletos* will actively seek solutions that would yield the maximum glory to Christ (Jn 16:14). This reality of the model may not be conducive to a leader whose agenda is to constantly reap praise, honor, and recognition upon the self. In fact, such a self-centered leader would be very uncomfortable with this

[12] Camillus, John C. 2008. "Strategy as a Wicked Problem." *Harvard Business Review*. May Issue.

aspect of the spiritual intuition model, due to its other-centered nature, and because they cannot control the outcome.

To recap, after the *Parakeletos* escorts a leader to a wicked problem, the Spirit essentially sifts the issues through the Logos. After the problem set is reduced to its basics, the *Parakeletos* actively seeks to bring maximum glory to Christ and will place such a solution within a leader's "gut" in the form of knowledge or wisdom. John 7:38 states it this way, "He who believes in Me, as the Scripture has said, out of his belly will flow rivers of living water." This flow of wisdom will become as real and factual to an influencer as empirical data are to a researcher. However, a wise leader understands the necessity of validating their spiritual intuition with the rigor of counting the cost. Luke 14:28–31 emphasizes this point by saying:

> For which of you, intending to build a tower, does not sit down first and count the cost, whether he has *enough* to finish *it*—[29] lest, after he has laid the foundation, and is not able to finish, all who see *it* begin to mock him,[30] saying, "This man began to build and was not able to finish."[31] Or what king, going to make war against another king, does not sit down first and consider whether he is able with ten thousand to meet him who comes against him with twenty thousand?

To this end, a leader takes the spiritual intuition and scrutinizes it with the conventional wisdom of the moment before employing a godly decision.

A GODLY INNER CIRCLE

Before the metaphorical trigger of choice unearthed within the spiritual intuition model is pulled, it would behoove a leader to seek out sound counsel and help from a team of trusted advisers. This circle of accountability can help to confirm or correct wisdom, as well as provide an added level of assurance in confronting the little foxes in our lives. In the sentiments of Proverbs 11:14, "Where *there is* no counsel, the people fall; But in the multitude of counselors *there is* safety." Failure, however, can be alleviated when counselors are granted permission to speak the truth without fear of retaliation and are allowed to hold a leader accountable. However, the opposite is also true when influencers believe they are the smartest person in the room and reject the wisdom of others. When this happens, as this book will demonstrate, the probability of that fox reaching maturity and spoiling future vineyards increases tremendously.

INSPIRATION

The final element of the LLF trap is inspiration. As the Latin epistemology of inspiration may suggest (i.e., *in*, to infuse, and *spirare*, breathe of life/spirit, or the act of exciting, influencing, or arousing another to action), one effective way to overcome a struggle is by sharing it with others. Luke 22:31–34 illustrates this point biblically when Jesus said,

> "Simon, Simon! Indeed, Satan has asked for you, that he may sift *you* as wheat.[32] But I have prayed for you, that your faith should not fail; and when you have returned to *Me*, strengthen your brethren."[33] But he said to Him, "Lord, I am ready to go with You, both to prison and to death."[34] Then He said, "I tell you, Peter, the rooster shall not crow this day before you will deny three times that you know Me."

In this passage, one discovers Jesus encouraging Peter after his denial and his return, to go and influence others with the good news of redemption. In a similar vein, it is essential to arouse others with the blood of the Lamb and the word of our testimony.

CONDUCT UNBECOMING

Unfortunately, King David's little leadership fox trap was either not activated or was not operating adequately. Such an assertion is made due to the troubling reality that a beloved king could be transformed into a narcissist. To recap a previous point, the king issued a provocative order to count the nation of Israel. What was the rationale for such a decision? David's own words are so that, "I may know *it*." Stated differently, the motive to know no longer had to do with pleasing or worshiping the Creator of the Universe who had placed him in that position (Psalm 75:6). David's desire to know no longer aligned with biblical protocol; as Exodus 30:12 reminds leaders that, "When you take the census of the children of Israel for their number, then every man shall give a ransom for himself to the LORD, when you number them, that there may be no plague among them when *you* number them." On the contrary, such an order had everything to do with stroking his ego (i.e., Edging God Out) and worshipping the metaphorical golden calf called "I." From the perspective of the divine, this business model can lead to an array of organizational issues (i.e., arrogance is the sin of idolatry—1 Sam 15:23) as this book will show.

In addition to the negative spiritual connotation of arrogance, emerging scientific research has demonstrated its impact on a leader. More specifically, Ian Robertson, author of *The Winner Effect*, suggests that when one tastes the effects of power, one receives a surge of testosterone, which in turn triggers the brain to release the pleasure chemical known as dopamine. Consequently, new-found power or victory can make a leader "smarter, more ambitious, more aggressive and more focused,"[13] as of a result of the surge of testosterone and dopamine. Such a reality can be a "good" thing if a leader remains balanced, but it can quickly become problematic when a leader becomes drunk with power. When this happens, more power can increase egocentricity, weaken a leader's ability to be empathic to others and can create a self-delusion that they are now above the rules.[14] Let us briefly examine how such attributes were manifest in the unbecoming conduct of the king.

> [3] And Joab answered, "May the LORD make His people a hundred times more than they are. But, my lord the king, *are* they not all my lord's servants? Why then does my lord require this thing? Why should he be a cause of guilt in Israel?"[4] Nevertheless, the king's word prevailed against Joab (1 Ch 21:3–4).

Empathy can be defined as, "having an understanding of and sensitivity to the feelings, thoughts, and situations of others. Empathy includes understanding another person's situation, experiencing the other person's emotions, and knowing his or her needs even though unstated."[15] As highlighted in the above verses, David was indifferent at best and unempathic at worst. For it was as if the king did not hear the three questions of Joab (which are affiliated to quadrant I of the BBLM) as revealed in his silence. Nevertheless, did his silence or gestures convey another message?

KING-THINK

Perhaps David's silence was an inverted form of groupthink? Groupthink is the tendency of highly cohesive groups to value consensus at the price of decision quality.[16] In this case, the group was an assembly of one—the king.

---

[13] Robertson, Ian H. 2012. *The Winner Effect: The Neuroscience of Succes and Failure.* New York, NY: Thomas Dunne Books. p. 130

[14] Ibid.

[15] McShane, Steven L., and MaryAnn V. Glinow. 2013. *Organizational Behavior: Emerging Knowledge. Global Reality [Kindle].* New York: McGraw-Hill Irwin. Loc. 3193.

[16] Ibid. Loc 7694.

In this book, this tendency is referred to as *king-think*, which is when a leader hides behind the positional and reverent power thrust upon them by legitimate authorities to superimpose selfish executive decisions designed to benefit themselves. Such leaders will utilize gamesmanship, fear, gestures, and (their preferred weapon of choice) the silent treatment, to advance their mission. According to Schneider (2014), this tactic is designed to

(1) Place the abuser in a position of control; (2) silence the target's attempts at assertion; (3) avoid conflict resolution/personal responsibility/compromise; or (4) punish the target for a perceived ego slight. Often, the result of the silent treatment is exactly what the person with narcissism wishes to create: a reaction from the target and a sense of control.[17]

If indeed king-think was in operation, and silence was the message preached from the figurative bully pulpit, then it would explain how "the king's word prevailed against Joab" without an additional sentence being spoken. Unfortunately, organizational leaders across the globe today are following suit and expecting maximum productivity from followers with a minimum explanation of the ethical "why."

BOARDROOM BOLDNESS CHATS

Who becomes the primary target when the adversary stands up against a nation, an organization, community, or even a home?

Solomon 2:15 encourages leaders to "Catch us the foxes, the little foxes that spoil vines." How can this be interpreted?

What are some examples of the little fox of the eyes, and do they have an impact on an organization's bottom line?

What are some examples of the little fox of the flesh and do they have an impact on an organization's bottom line?

What are some examples of the little fox of the pride of life and do they have an impact on an organization's bottom line?

What is the leadership little fox trap and which element is the most important?

What is *king-think* and how does such a trait impact an organization?

---

[17]Schneider, Andrea. 2014. *Silent Treatment: Preferred Weapon of People with Narcissism.* June 2. Accessed March 12, 2017. http://www.goodtherapy.org/blog/silent-treatment-a-narcissistic-persons-preferred-weapon-0602145

CHAPTER 2

Decoding the Silence

It may be true that the king's word prevailed against Joab but what about the rest of the royal court? More specifically, why didn't anyone else try to break through the narcissistic behavior of the monarch and the barriers of king-think for the sake of the nation? Was not the royal court filled with accomplished and talented servants of the state as delineated in 2 Samuel 8:15–18, 2 Samuel 20:23–26 and 1 Chronicles 18:14–17? Where were the mighty men like Benaiah who struck down Moab's mighty warriors and also went down into a pit on a snowy day to kill a lion (1 Chr 11:22)? Why didn't Queen Bathsheba, Mephibosheth, Solomon, or any other court attendant act? In a similar line of inquiry, what keeps organizational citizens in the twenty-first century quiet in the face of corrupt practices in the boardroom? (Fig. 2.1).

The literature offers an array of logical explanations to the above the questions. Ryan and Oestreich's (1998) research, to illustrate, found that 70 percent of the people in the workforce were hesitant to confront a leader due to the fear factor. Additionally, Scott (2004) asserts that there may be other variables that muzzle followers, which include: (1) the concern of being labeled a troublemaker; (2) being perceived as not being a team player; (3) concerns revolving around the loss of salary; and (4) not wanting to fall out of favor with the boss.[1] Perhaps one the leading

---

[1] Scott, Nancy R. 2004. *How to Confront the Boss and Win.* Accessed March 14, 2017. http://www.nancyscott.com/page50/page33/page33.html

---

© The Author(s) 2018
M. A. Buford, *Bold Followership*, Christian Faith Perspectives in Leadership and Business, https://doi.org/10.1007/978-3-319-74530-5_2

19

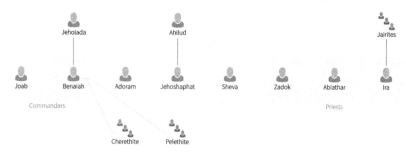

Fig. 2.1 King David's royal court

reasons why some people do not speak out is due to the lack of knowledge and prudent boldness?

THE MORAL IMPERATIVE

If one of the causations of organizational silence in the face of wrong is the lack of knowledge or boldness, then perhaps the sentiments of the Drum Major of Justice may be the first step in helping an influencer successfully navigate the troubling waters of questionable orders. Martin Luther King Jr. in *The Letter from Birmingham Jail* skillfully asks:

> How can you advocate breaking some laws and obeying others? The answer lies in the fact that there are two types of laws: just and unjust. I would be the first to advocate obeying just laws. One has not only a legal but a moral responsibility to obey just laws. Conversely, one has a moral responsibility to disobey unjust laws. I would agree with St. Augustine that "an unjust law is no law at all." Now, what is the difference between the two? How does one determine whether a law is just or unjust? A just law is a man-made code that squares with the moral law or the law of God. An unjust law is a code that is out of harmony with the moral law. To put in the terms of St. Thomas Aquinas: An unjust law is a human law that is not rooted in eternal law and natural law. Any law that uplifts human personality is just. A law that degrades human personality is unjust.[2]

---

[2] Martin Luther King Jr. 1963. "Letter from Birmingham Jail." *The Estate of Martin Luther King Jr.* April 16. Accessed March 14, 2017. http://kingencyclopedia.stanford.edu/kingweb/popular.requests/frequentdocs/birmingham.pdf

If one were to apply the above sentiment to David's order to count the nation of Israel, one would find issues. Specifically, a reasonable person would have to conclude that such a directive was a clear endeavor to prevent God's people from working out the reality of being fearfully and wonderfully made in God's image (Ps 139:14) to a being marginalized as a mere number. This total disregard for life in the name of vainglory is enough fuel to fan the flames of the moral imperative to speak. Moreover, this rule of thumb (i.e., just and unjust laws) can provide a person with a philosophical framework to discern the morality of orders.

CORPORATE PRESSURE

Before a more in-depth conversation is offered around the employment of individual moral imperatives (i.e., apples), one must acknowledge the gripping power that an organizational climate (i.e., the apple barrel) has upon her citizens. One of the most provocative experiments conducted in America illustrates this point, the famous Milgram experiment, which demonstrates how good people can do evil things. More specifically, Stanley Milgram designed a study that endeavored to explore the question, "Could it be that Eichmann and his million accomplices in the Holocaust were just following orders? Could we call them all accomplices?"[3] To answer this question, Stanley recruited participants through a newspaper and paid them $4.50.

The participants were told that they were randomly selected to be either the teacher or the learner. However, the study rigged the selection so that the participant would always be the teacher. Once the roles were established the student, who was a person privy to the study, was strapped into a chair with what appeared to be electrodes, in the presence of the participant. With a divider between the student and the teacher, the teacher was instructed to gradually increase the volts administered to the student. The experimenter in a white coat, which became a symbol of authority, would direct the teacher to continue the intensity of the shocks. Even in the face of uncertainty, the teacher was instructed by the experimenter to "please continue" or "you have no other choice to continue" (Fig. 2.2). According to McLeod (2007),

---

[3] Milgram, Stanley. 1974. *Obedience to authority*. Harper Collins.

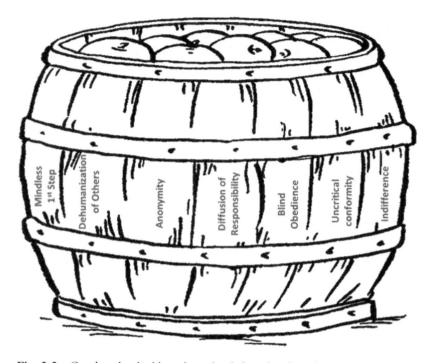

Fig. 2.2 Good apples, bad barrels, and ugly barrel makers, based on Zimbardo's (2008) "Psychology of Evil" Ted Talk

65% (two-thirds) of participants (i.e., teachers) continued to the highest level of 450 volts. All the participants continued to 300 volts. Ordinary people are likely to follow orders given by an authority figure, even to the extent of killing an innocent human being. Obedience to authority is ingrained in us all from the way we are brought up. People tend to obey orders from other people if they recognize their authority as morally right and or legally based...[4].

GOOD APPLES, BAD BARRELS, AND UGLY BARREL MAKERS

In a similar vein as the Milgram experiment, the Stanford Prison Experiment conducted by Phil Zimbardo confirms the fact that bad barrels can potentially spoil good apples and that the makers of the barrel are even more

[4] McLeod, Saul. 2007. *The Milgram Experiment*. Accessed August 27, 2017. www.simplypsychology.org/milgram.html

liable. Stated differently, after designing an experiment to explore the effects that institutional pressure can have on a person, willing participants were solicited from the population to function in a mock prison scenario. Upon being screened for suitability for the study, the participants were randomly selected to be either a prisoner or a guard, with Zimbardo functioning as the superintendent. Although the participants agreed to engage in the 14-day experiment at $15 a day, it was terminated after six days because of the appalling behavior of every actor within the study.

In the final analysis, this study confirmed that situational factors are a greater predictor of a mishap than individual variables.[5] Zimbardo (2008) elaborates on the conditions that set the stage for evil to triumph. More specifically, Zimbardo refers to such environments as the seven social processes that grease the slippery slope of evil. As depicted in Figure 2.2, the first social gesture is to take the first small step mindlessly. In the context of David's royal court, this behavior would be akin to immediately counting every person around the city of David without reservation or internal dissonance. In the case of the Milgram experiment, this unprocessed first step was the willingness to electrocute another human being, who had done no wrong, at the command of an authority figure. The second progression revolves around the dehumanization of others. In the scenario of David, his momentary lapse of judgment caused him to no longer see the nation as being fearfully and wonderfully made in the image of God. On the contrary, king-thinking reduced God's people to a statistic or a mere number. In like manner, participants in the Stanford Prison Experiment were stripped of their identity and were referred to as prisoner #8612.

The third element of Zimbardo's (2008) model was the notion of the de-individuation of self. De-individuation can be defined as the loss of a person's sense of individuality and personal responsibility. This mindset can be displayed in David's overall demeanor when he hid behind the trappings of the crown. Seemingly, the heaviness affiliated with this position seduced him into forgetting that God had raised him from being a shepherd. This same issue can be found in the mannerisms of the participants of the Stanford Prison Experiment. More specifically, the uniforms prescribed for the guards included identical khaki uniforms, whistles around the neck, Billy clubs, and sunglasses. Although the shades were designed to keep the prisoners from making eye contact, it also contributed to the anonymity of the actors.

[5] Haney, C., Banks, W., and Zimbardo, P. 1973. "A Study of Prisoners and Guards in a Simulated Prison." *Naval Research Review, 30* 4–17.

The diffusion of personal responsibility is the fourth element on the progression model. At this point, a person convinces themselves that they are no longer accountable for their actions. On the occasion of David's decision point, this is an oxymoron. It is a contradiction because David's position as king implied that the metaphorical buck stopped with him, but his behavior conveyed just the opposite. One can see this trait in operation within the Milgram experiment. More specifically, 65 percent of the participants in this study continued to the highest level of volts, and all proceeded to 300 volts because they believed someone else would assume responsibility for their actions.[6] This sad reality has contributed to an array of organizational mishaps and to the growing body of literature on ethical calamities.

The fifth element that contributes to a toxic culture is a blind allegiance to authority. The natural propensity of outsiders observing such a phenomenon is to ask why would one aimlessly follow such a toxic personality. Lipman-Blumen (2005) suggests that a follower's psychological need to be kept safe, the need to feel special, a desire to have a seat at the community table, and the need for reassuring authority figures to fill our parent's shoes may be likely causations.[7] If Lipman-Blumen's observation is correct, then it provides a logical explanation for the silence in the king's court and the passive behavior of the participants in an array of similar entities.

The uncritical conformity to group norms is the sixth element of Zimbardo's (2008) model. Perhaps this point can be illustrated best by a funny episode from the television show Candid Camera in which a group of actors would enter an elevator to explore whether group pressure could influence the behavior of a random person taking an elevator from one floor to another. Once the random person entered the elevator, the group of actors would simultaneously perform a task such as turning around, removing hats, or putting hats back on. Without exception, the participants in the episode would conform to outrageous gestures simply because they perceived it to be normal. In other words, they were caught on candid camera because they suspended their ability to question and analyze the situation critically. Regrettably, and in a not so humorous fashion, this element has contributed to an array of moral incidents.

The final and perhaps the most troubling component of the progression model is indifference. The passive tolerance of evil through inaction

---

[6]McLeod, Saul. 2007. *The Milgram Experiment.* Accessed August 27, 2017. www.simplypsychology.org/milgram.html

[7]Lipman-Blumen, Jean. 2005. *The Allure of Toxic Leaders.* New York: Oxford University Press. p. 29.

Fig. 2.3 The seven factors of a spiritual organization

can be seen in almost every ethical mishap in history. One can see indifference in the behavior of David's court, in participants of the Stanford Prison Experiment, and in countries like genocide-stricken Rwanda. One can argue at this point that the manufacturers of evil understand this dynamic and often seek to exploit the inaction of the masses. Hence, "All that is required for evil to triumph is for good people to do nothing" (Fig. 2.3).

Reverse Engineering the Barrel

The Merriam-Webster dictionary has an interesting definition of the phrase reverse engineering. It means to disassemble and examine or analyze in detail (a product or device) to discover the concepts involved in manufacture, usually to produce something similar. Considering such a meaning, the question becomes, "If one were to reverse engineer Zimbardo's (2008) findings on the ugly barrel, what positive organizational attributes can be gleaned to build a healthier climate?" As illustrated in Figure 2.3, there are seven factors of a spiritual organization. In an oxymoronic manner, such aspects were displayed in the life of David before his narcissistic moment as recorded in 1 Chronicles 21:1–2.

PRAYERFUL FIRST STEP

Now it happened, when David and his men came to Ziklag, on the third day, that the Amalekites had invaded the South and Ziklag, attacked Ziklag and burned it with fire,[2] and had taken captive the women and those who were there, from small to great; they did not kill anyone, but carried them away and went their way.[3] So David and his men came to the city, and there it was, burned with fire; and their wives, their sons, and their daughters had been taken captive.[4] Then David and the people who were with him lifted up their voices and wept, until they had no more power to weep.[5] And David's two wives, Ahinoam the Jezreelitess, and Abigail the widow of Nabal the Carmelite, had been taken captive.[6] Now David was greatly distressed, for the people spoke of stoning him, because the soul of all the people was grieved, every man for his sons and his daughters. But David strengthened himself in the LORD his God.[7] Then David said to Abiathar the priest, Ahimelech's son, "Please bring the ephod here to me." And Abiathar brought the ephod to David.[8] So David inquired of the LORD, saying, "Shall I pursue this troop? Shall I overtake them?"And He answered him, "Pursue, for you shall surely overtake them and without fail recover all." (1 Sa 30:1–8)

In this biblical extract, one discovers David and his men returning to Ziklag after a three-day mission to find the camp in flames and their families missing. This drastic scene momentarily created an atmosphere of grief and sparked a campaign to have David stoned. But David, as the scripture indicates, tapped into his spirituality and obtained strength from the Lord. After David recalibrated himself, he requested that Abiathar the priest bring him the ephod. According to Elwell and Comfort (2001) the ephod was an, "Upper garment worn during religious services associated with the tabernacle or temple. 'Ephod' generally referred to the ornamented vest that the high priest wore over a blue robe (Ex 28:31). Included with the ephod were the Urim and Thummim, the sacred lots."[8] Moreover, Elwell and Comfort suggest that the ephod served as a means of revelation from God, especially concerning military operations.

Stated slightly differently, before David took a mindless, and possibly an emotional, first step, the son of Jesse prayed a specific organizational prayer—*Shall I pursue this troop and shall I overtake them?* Instead of caving into fear-based thinking that would have seemingly undermined the entire mission, David consulted the truth (Jn 14:6). It was as if such

---

[8] Elwell, W. A., & Comfort, P. W. (2001). In *Tyndale Bible dictionary* (p. 437). Wheaton, IL: Tyndale House Publishers.

inquiring was David's way to invoke Proverbs 3:5–6, "Trust in the LORD with all your heart, And lean not on your own understanding; In all your ways acknowledge Him, And He shall direct your paths." This practice of acknowledging, or praying, in the end became the ultimate competitive advantage due to the divine revelation received. As such, instead of entities in the twenty-first century exhausting an overwhelming amount of capital to solve complex problems, perhaps executives can learn to embrace the practice of President Abraham Lincoln when he said, "I have been driven many times upon my knees by the overwhelming conviction that I had nowhere else to go. My own wisdom and that of all about me seemed insufficient for that day."

THE PLATINUM RULE

Now David said, "Is there still anyone who is left of the house of Saul, that I may show him kindness for Jonathan's sake?"[2] And there was a servant of the house of Saul whose name was Ziba. So when they had called him to David, the king said to him, "Are you Ziba?" He said, "At your service!"[3] Then the king said, "Is there not still someone of the house of Saul, to whom I may show the kindness of God?" And Ziba said to the king, "There is still a son of Jonathan who is lame in his feet."[4] So the king said to him, "Where is he?" And Ziba said to the king, "Indeed he is in the house of Machir the son of Ammiel, in Lo Debar.[5] Then King David sent and brought him out of the house of Machir the son of Ammiel, from Lo Debar.[6] Now when Mephibosheth the son of Jonathan, the son of Saul, had come to David, he fell on his face and prostrated himself. Then David said, "Mephibosheth?" And he answered, "Here is your servant!"[7] So David said to him, "Do not fear, for I will surely show you kindness for Jonathan your father's sake, and will restore to you all the land of Saul your grandfather; and you shall eat bread at my table continually." (2 Sa 9:1–7)

Bruce Winston made a compelling case for agapao love in *Be a Leader for God's Sake*. Such an argument was predicated on two premises. First, that agapao is a moral love that "means that today's leaders must consider the human and spiritual aspects of their employees/followers. The people working for you are not just flesh and blood who respond to wages as a mule responds to a carrot on a stick. Your employees are complete people with physical, mental, and spiritual needs."[9] Second, Winston contends

---

[9] Winston, Bruce. 2002. *Be a Leader for God's Sake.* Virgina Beach, VA: Regent University-School of Leadership Studies. pp. 8–9.

this form of love can best be described as the Platinum Rule, "Do unto others as they want you to do unto them." (Note: the Golden Rule states, "Do unto others as you would have them do unto you.") A shining example of David implementing the Platinum Rule in the culture can be found in 2 Samuel 9:1–7. Contextually speaking Saul and his sons died. However, before their death, Jonathan treated David extremely kindly. Such kindness could have been perceived as an act of treason, or the ultimate act of disrespect, because Saul had treated David as an enemy. Regardless of the disdain, David actively searched out an occasion to bless the lineage of Jonathan by asking, "Is there still anyone who is left of the house of Saul, that I may show him kindness for Jonathan's sake?" That person happened to be Mephibosheth who was lame. When David summoned Mephibosheth he seemingly treated him the way he would have wanted—he was kind, restored his land, and gave him a permanent place at the king's table. This second factor of a spiritual organization has been empirically validated as the leading way to elevate trust in a team.[10]

TRANSPARENCY

Now the acts of King David, first and last, indeed they are written in the book of Samuel the seer, in the book of Nathan the prophet, and in the book of Gad the seer,[30] with all his reign and his might, and the events that happened to him, to Israel, and to all the kingdoms of the lands. (1 Ch 29:29–30)

The third factor of a spiritual organization is transparency. Covey (2006, p. 464) indicates that transparency is "about being open. It is about being real and genuine and telling the truth in a way people can verify. It is based on the principles of honesty, openness, integrity, and authenticity."[11] As indicated in 1 Chronicles 29:29–30 the acts of David were recorded in a very open and transparent manner, which others could verify. Such openness extended not only to the king but also to Israel and all the kingdoms of the land. This small but profound gesture of openness can make the difference between a good organization and one that is operating at the level of greatness.

[10]Zak, Paul J. 2017. *Trust Factor.* New York: AMACOM. Loc 1713 Kindle.
[11]Covey, Stephen. 2006. *The Speed of Trust.* New York: FREE PRESS.

DECODING THE SILENCE   29

ACCOUNTABILITY

Have mercy upon me, O God, According to Your loving kindness; According to the multitude of Your tender mercies, Blot out my transgressions. Wash me thoroughly from my iniquity, And cleanse me from my sin. For I acknowledge my transgressions, And my sin is always before me. Against You, You only, have I sinned. And done this evil in Your sight—That You may be found just when You speak, And blameless when You judge. Behold, I was brought forth in iniquity, And in sin my mother conceived me. Behold, You desire truth in the inward parts, And in the hidden part You will make me to know wisdom. Purge me with hyssop, and I shall be clean; Wash me, and I shall be whiter than snow. Make me hear joy and gladness, That the bones You have broken may rejoice. Hide Your face from my sins, And blot out all my iniquities. Create in me a clean heart, O God And renew a steadfast spirit within me. Do not cast me away from Your presence, And do not take Your Holy Spirit from me. Restore to me the joy of Your salvation, And uphold me by Your generous Spirit. Then I will teach transgressors Your ways, And sinners shall be converted to You (Ps 51:1—13).

In a complementary manner to transparency, the fourth factor of a spiritual organization is accountability. Again, Steven Covey's insight holds true when he declared that "accountability is about holding yourself as well as others accountable. It's about taking responsibility for results, being careful on how you'll communicate how you're doing and how others are doing. Accountability doesn't avoid or shirk responsibility nor do they blame others or point fingers when things go wrong."[12] As highlighted in the above text, David provides a template for assuming responsibility and being accountable. After sinning against God by committing adultery with Bathsheba and having her husband murdered, the son of Jesse does not point any fingers, nor does he try to shift the blame to others. On the contrary, for this act David stands tall and declares, "For I acknowledge my transgressions, and my sin is always before me. Against You, You only, have I sinned. And done this evil in Your sight." This courageous act may not necessarily be the most popular course of action in today's context but it is the godly way. For David best summarizes it al in Psalm 18:30 through the leading of the Holy Spirit, "*As for* God, His way *is* perfect; The word of the LORD is proven; He *is* a shield to all who trust in Him." So instead of protecting our endeavors with the instrument of

---

[12] Ibid. p. 310.

30 M. A. BUFORD

diffusion of personal responsibility, perhaps it would be a more logical approach to allow the truth to be our shield.

MORAL LOYALTY

Now it happened, when Saul had returned from following the Philistines, that it was told him, saying, "Take note! David is in the Wilderness of En Gedi."[2] Then Saul took three thousand chosen men from all Israel, and went to seek David and his men on the Rocks of the Wild Goats.[3] So he came to the sheepfolds by the road, where there was a cave; and Saul went in to attend to his needs. (David and his men were staying in the recesses of the cave.)[4] Then the men of David said to him, "This is the day of which the LORD said to you, 'Behold, I will deliver your enemy into your hand, that you may do to him as it seems good to you.' " And David arose and secretly cut off a corner of Saul's robe.[5] Now it happened afterward that David's heart troubled him because he had cut Saul's robe.[6] And he said to his men, "The LORD forbid that I should do this thing to my master, the LORD's anointed, to stretch out my hand against him, seeing he is the anointed of the LORD."[7] So David restrained his servants with these words, and did not allow them to rise against Saul. And Saul got up from the cave and went on his way.[8] David also arose afterward, went out of the cave, and called out to Saul, saying, "My lord the king!" And when Saul looked behind him, David stooped with his face to the earth, and bowed down.[9] And David said to Saul: "Why do you listen to the words of men who say, 'Indeed David seeks your harm'?[10] Look, this day your eyes have seen that the LORD delivered you today into my hand in the cave, and someone urged me to kill you. But my eye spared you, and I said, 'I will not stretch out my hand against my lord, for he is the LORD's anointed.'[11] Moreover, my father, see! Yes, see the corner of your robe in my hand! For in that I cut off the corner of your robe, and did not kill you, know and see that there is neither evil nor rebellion in my hand, and I have not sinned against you. Yet you hunt my life to take it. (I Sa 24:1—11)

The fifth factor of a spiritual organization is having moral loyalty to the institution. A careful analysis 1 Samuel 24:1–11 will showcase David's allegiance, not to a person (i.e., Saul) but to the position or institution (i.e., the Kingdom of God). Before David ascended the throne, Saul's jealousy spurred him to pursue David with the objective of killing him. As outlined above, this account indicates that Saul took three battalions of choice men to complete the mission. In the course of providential events, Saul enters the cave David and his men were in to "attend to his needs." While there, David's men essentially encouraged him to seize the moment for they believed that the Lord was handing Saul into the hands of David.

After David cut a piece from Saul's robe, his heart got convicted, seemingly due to his moral loyalty to God. David clearly understood the caution of 1 Chronicles 16:20–22, "When they went from one nation to another, And from *one* kingdom to another people, He permitted no man to do them wrong; Yes, He rebuked kings for their sakes, *Saying*, Do not touch My anointed ones, And do My prophets no harm." Even though Saul had no just cause or reason to take out David, he wrongfully pursued him. In a similar vein, David had every right to defend his life, particularly under such conditions. Nevertheless, David understood the principles of moral loyalty. Namely, allegiance to the principles of the institution (in this case the Kingdom of God) outranks devotion to an individual. In this case, God's law required that no man should touch God's anointed (even if the anointed one, like Saul, is in the wrong) nor do His prophets harm. Thus, it is better to suffer for moral loyalty than to exercise blind obedience to a person.

ORGANIZATIONAL LEARNING

Again David gathered all the choice men of Israel, thirty thousand.² And David arose and went with all the people who were with him from Baale Judah to bring up from there the ark of God, whose name is called by the Name, the LORD *of Hosts, who dwells between the cherubim.³ So they set the ark of God on a new cart, and brought it out of the house of Abinadab, which was on the hill; and Uzzah and Ahio, the sons of Abinadab, drove the new cart.⁴ And they brought it out of the house of Abinadab, which was on the hill, accompanying the ark of God; and Ahio went before the ark.⁵ Then David and all the house of Israel played music before the* LORD *on all kinds of instruments of fir wood, on harps, on stringed instruments, on tambourines, on sistrums, and on cymbals.⁶ And when they came to Nachon's threshing floor, Uzzah put out his hand to the ark of God and took hold of it, for the oxen stumbled.⁷ Then the anger of the* LORD *was aroused against Uzzah, and God struck him there for his error; and he died there by the ark of God.⁸ And David became angry because of the* LORD'*s outbreak against Uzzah; and he called the name of the place Perez Uzzah to this day.⁹ David was afraid of the* LORD *that day; and he said, "How can the ark of the* LORD *come to me?" [emphasis mine.]¹⁰ So David would not move the ark of the* LORD *with him into the City of David; but David took it aside into the house of Obed-Edom the Gittite.¹¹ The ark of the* LORD *remained in the house of Obed-Edom the Gittite three months. And the* LORD *blessed Obed-Edom and all his household.¹² Now it was told King David, saying, "The* LORD *has blessed the house of Obed-Edom and all that belongs to him, because of the ark of God." So David went and brought up the ark of God from the house of Obed-Edom to the*

32   M. A. BUFORD

City of David with gladness.[13] And so it was, when those bearing the ark of the LORD had gone six paces, that he sacrificed oxen and fatted sheep.[14] Then David danced before the LORD with all his might; and David was wearing a linen ephod.[15] So David and all the house of Israel brought up the ark of the LORD with shouting and with the sound of the trumpet. (2 Sa 6:1—15)

David's question (emphasized above), points toward the sixth factor of a spiritual unit. Namely, upon the king convening a symposium with 30,000 choice men to understand the best method to move the ark of the Lord, a decision was made to place it upon a new cart to be towed by oxen. Such a choice would prove to be problematic because no one forecast the ensuing mishap. As a result, Uzzah in his zeal made a reactionary and fatal decision to hold up the ark with his hands as it stumbled. As a result, Uzzah's life was taken by God, and the operation came to a halt. One can argue that this incident occurred due to Peter Senge's notion of learning disabilities (LD) of an entity. More specifically, there are two LDs that seemingly align with this point. The first is the illusion of taking charge. This is where managers spring into action in an outward, proactive manner, without conducting an internal analysis to understand the required changes needed to properly sustain a proposed transformation.[13] The second LD that seemingly contributed to the incident was being unaware of slow, gradual processes that present greater threats than immediate events.

Although such LDs may have contributed to the calamity, David in this context employed the traits of a learning organization to correct the course. Namely, 2 Samuel 6:9 indicates that "David was afraid of the Lord that day." The Hebrew, יָרֵא, יָרֵא *yare'* /yaw·**ray**/,[14] a translation of the word afraid, can also be interpreted as inspiring reverence. From a biblical point of view, there is a positive relationship between reverencing God and self-mastery. Proverbs 1:7 indicates that the fear of the Lord is the beginning of knowledge. As such, this fresh reverence of the Lord seemingly sparked a corporate renewal of self-discipline and a personal knowledge of the Lord. Peter Senge refers to this phenomenon as personal mastery. The theory of the first aspect of a learning organization is that an organization cannot go beyond the learning of its individual citizens. To this end, it is critical for entities to encourage learning at the personal level.

[13] Pugh, Derek S, and David J Hickson. 2000. *Great Writers on Organizations.* Burlington: Ashgate Publishing Limited.

[14] Strong, J. (1995). *Enhanced Strong's Lexicon.* Woodside Bible Fellowship.

The second feature of Peter Senge's notion of organizational learning is mental models. At this point, Senge contends that a continual challenge of entrenched personal belief systems should be explored. Without this process, biases or unprocessed worldviews may inadvertently undermine business deliberations. Perhaps the most effective tools for unearthing one's mental model are probing and relevant questions. This is precisely the methodology that David used when he pondered, "How can the ark of the Lord come to me?" This question seemingly forced both the choice men and David to confront their mental models. Perhaps the most pervasive and collective mindset that undermined the entire process was the belief that God's ark should be moved around on the assumptions of men. Stated differently, the mental model of transporting the ark of the Lord with oxen seemed to overthrow biblical principles.

The third discipline of a Senge learning organization is the building of a shared vision. This futuristic picture of possibilities is the metaphorical fuel that energizes a corporation to exceed expectations. It is not enough for a leader to cast the vision, though this is key, everyone within the organization must also see it, and be willing to seize it. In the case of David, the people began to see the endless possibilities when they noticed how "The LORD has blessed the house of Obed-Edom and all that belongs to him, because of the ark of God." (2 Sa 6:12) It was as if the reality of the blessing of the Lord upon the house of Obed-Edom sparked an urgency within the hearts of the people to bring to pass such a possibility in the city of David.

Once this sneak preview of tomorrow's promises is embraced, the fourth element of a learning organization can be implemented. Namely, a commitment to team learning can spur a team to greatness. At this place "an open dialogue of cooperation in groups, rather than 'turf battles' [become the norm.] Only then can the intelligence of the team exceed that of its members."[15] This is exactly what happened after a shared vision inspired the people. It was as if they collectively learned from the death of Uzzah, did not allow tribal turf wars to emerge, and employed team learning to solve wicked problems. It would be a logical inference to suggest that this new-found team knowledge is what escorted them to the Levitical law concerning the ark of God. Specifically, the team may have rediscovered the truths outlined in Numbers 4:15 that only the Levites should carry (not be driven by oxen). It indicates that "when Aaron and his sons

---

[15] Pugh, Derek S, and David J Hickson. 2000. *Great Writers on Organizations*. Burlington: Ashgate Publishing Limited. p. 284.

34   M. A. BUFORD

have finished covering the sanctuary and all the furnishings of the sanctuary when the camp is set to go, then the sons of Kohath shall come to carry *them;* but they shall not touch any holy thing, lest they die. These *are* the things in the tabernacle of meeting which the sons of Kohath are to carry."

The fifth discipline, and perhaps the one that provides the most leverage, is systems thinking. This is the unifying moment in the life of an organization that propels a firm to the next level. However, as teams build on this discipline, it is understood that "today's problems come from yesterday's solutions."[16] As such, it was the nation of Israel's yesterday solution of allowing the ark to remain at the house of Abinadab that created the conditions for movement. Thus, systems thinking prevailed as they carried the ark in the prescribed biblical manner and made a sacrifice of praise after the organization took six steps.

BOLD FOLLOWERSHIP

The final element of a spiritual organization is bold followership. Because the remaining chapters will be dedicated to describing a detailed boardroom model for followers, the reader's attention at this point will be focused on a variable known as boldness. Manser (2009) suggested that boldness is ultimately an inner confidence that permeates from God, which enables one to accomplish a task courageously or to engage a person.[17] Although there are an array of scriptures that undergird this understanding of boldness, the passages outlined in Table 2.1 will shape the ensuing

Table 2.1   The biblical source of boldness

Passage	*Narration*
Proverbs 28:1	The wicked flees when no one is pursuing, but the **righteous** are as **bold** as a lion
Psalm 138:3	In the day I **cried out**, you answered and made me bold with strength in my soul
Acts 4:13	Now when they saw the boldness of Peter and John, and perceived that they were uneducated and untrained men, they marveled. And they realized that they had **been with Jesus**
Revelation 21:8	But the **cowardly**, unbelieving, abominable, murderers, sexually immoral, sorcerers, idolaters, and all liars shall have their part in the lake which burns with fire and brimstone, which is the second death

[16] Ibid.

[17] Manser, M. H. (2009). *Dictionary of Bible Themes: The Accessible and Comprehensive Tool for Topical Studies.* London: Martin Manser.

discussion and help to answer the question, "Do the scriptures provide a practical template to cultivate courage in the twenty-first century?"

THE RIGHTEOUSNESS FACTOR

In an endeavor to devise a plausible answer to the above inquiry, the wisdom abstracted from Proverbs 28:1 should be considered. Namely, the righteous are as bold as a lion. The Hebrew term for righteous, צַדִּיק *tsaddiq*, can be translated as just, innocent, in the right or upright. When a person resides in righteousness, the lion-like virtue of boldness rises within the being of a leader. Debatably, there are three components of *tsaddiq*. The first component can be categorized as tactical righteousness, which points toward a just individual living their daily life as an upstanding citizen who may suddenly be faced with a personal ethical dilemma. Should the single mother of two children lie about her taxes so that she can get a larger return to help out her struggling family or should she report with integrity? On the contrary, this single mother understands what it means to be just, models justice, and teaches her children to do the right thing. As such, this virtuous woman, struggling to stay afloat, believes that God will continue to supply all of her needs according to His riches in glory by Christ Jesus (Phil 4:19).

The second component of the model can be described as operational righteousness. Operational *tsaddiq* is when an innocent actor happens upon a problematic moment, and they lean in to positively impact the situation, even in the face of suffering, threat, or the loss of life. Two exemplars, albeit on different spectrums of this virtue, are Rosa Parks and William Kyle Carpenter. Consider the Medal of Honor recipient's citation first:

> *For conspicuous gallantry and intrepidity at the risk of his life above and beyond the call of duty while serving as an automatic rifleman with Company F, 2nd Battalion, 9th Marines, Regimental Combat Team One, 1st Marine Division (Forward), 1st Marine Expeditionary Force (Forward), in Helmand Province, Afghanistan in support of Operation Enduring Freedom on 21 November, 2010. Lance Corporal Carpenter was a member of a platoon-sized coalition force comprised of two reinforced Marine rifle squads, partnered with an Afghan National Army squad. The platoon had established Patrol Base Dakota two days earlier in a small village in the Marja District in order to disrupt enemy activity and provide security for the local Afghan population.*
>
> *Lance Corporal Carpenter and a fellow Marine were manning a rooftop security position on the perimeter of Patrol Base Dakota when the enemy initiated*

36   M. A. BUFORD

a daylight attack with hand grenades, one of which landed inside their sand-bagged position. Without hesitation and with complete disregard for his own safety, Lance Corporal Carpenter moved towards the grenade in an attempt to shield his fellow Marine from the deadly blast. When the grenade detonated, his body absorbed the brunt of the blast, severely wounding him but saving the life of his fellow Marine. By his undaunted courage, bold fighting spirit, and unwavering devotion to duty in the face of almost certain death, Lance Corporal Carpenter reflected great credit upon himself and upheld the highest traditions of the Marine Corps and the United States Naval Service.

As indicated in the above citation, without hesitation, and with complete disregard for his safety, Lance Corporal Carpenter moved toward the grenade to shield his fellow Marine's life. What the citation does not capture, however, is Carpenter's form of righteousness that enabled him to exercise lion-like boldness. In an interview with Fox news, Carpenter was questioned about a tattoo on his body. Ironically, in spite of the damage caused by the grenade, this tattoo remained intact. In his response, he mentioned that the tattoo was, "Out of the book of Psalm and it says, 'Blessed be the Lord my Rock, Who trains my hands for war, And my fingers for battle…' That absolutely pertained to me and fellow Marines fighting to left and right of me. We all understood that it was a good chance that many of us would not make it back… I am a believer and knew that over there I would need my faith." Lance Corporal Carpenter's faith became his righteousness, as described in 2 Corinthians 5:14, which empowered him to exercise conspicuous gallantry and intrepidity at the risk of his life.

At the other end of the operational courage spectrum is Rosa Park. This Presidential Medal of Freedom recipient citation indicates that

On December 1, 1955, going home from work, Rosa Parks boarded a city bus in Montgomery, Alabama, and with one modest act of defiance, changed the course of history. By refusing to give up her seat, she sparked the Montgomery bus boycott and helped launch the civil rights movement. In the years since, she remained committed to the cause of freedom, speaking out against injustice here and abroad. Called the "first lady of civil rights," Rosa Parks has demonstrated, in the words of Robert Kennedy, that each time a person strikes out against injustice, she sends forth a tiny ripple of hope which, crossing millions of others, can sweep down the walls of oppression.

As noted above, Rosa Parks refused to give up her seat. But what was the source of the strength in the first lady of the Civil Rights movement to make such a bold gesture? In her own words, "I felt the Lord would give me the strength to endure whatever I had to face. God did away with all my fear... It was time for someone to stand up—or, in my case, sit down. I refused to move."[18]

Strategic righteousness is the third element of the model. Strategic *tsaddiq* occurs when the highest level of an organization decides to stand "in the right" and are willing to assume the risks affiliated with such a position, regardless of the price. A shining example of this principle is President Abraham Lincoln's decision at Fort Sumter. History indicates that on December 20, 1860, South Carolina seceded from the Union. Such a move, primarily championed by the newly elected president of the Confederate States of America, would set the conditions for civil war due to the disputed ownership of Fort Sumter. Should the fort now belong to the South, based on the premise of separation, or is it a Union asset that should be defended? This was Lincoln's dilemma as he pondered his options. Should he abandon the fort? A course of action that would undoubtedly give credence to the South's cause. Should he employ naval forces to resupply the fort? This path would surely look like Northern aggression and would arguably remove the righteousness factor. What was Lincoln's choice? A righteous one, to resupply using a naval convoy.[19] This non-threatening decision positioned the Union *in the right* and painted Jefferson Davis' Confederacy as the aggressor when they attacked Fort Sumter. This notion of being *in the right* is the very argument that earned him the presidency when he concluded his address at the Cooper Union Address on February 27, 1860, by saying, "Let us have faith that right makes might, and in that faith, let us, to the end, dare to do our duty as we understand it."

The Choke Factor

The common denominator of the exemplars of tactical, operational, and strategic righteousness was indeed that right makes might, as illustrated in Psalms 138:3 and Acts 4:13. These passages, depicted in Table 2.1, highlight the relationship between petitioning God in prayer, walking daily

---

[18] Associated Press. 1995. *Civil Rights Pioneer's Book Tells Impact of Religion: History.* January 21. Accessed September 23, 2017. www.articles.latimes/1995-01-21/local/me-22523_1_civil-rights-movement

[19] Bunch, Lonnie. 2011. "The Washington Post." *Who's To blame for the first shot.* April 10. Accessed September 23, 2017. https://www.washingtonpost.com/lifestyle/style/who-is-to-blame-for-first-shot/2011/04/04/AF1M5uHD_story.html?utm_term=.19b0bc63aba7

with the Lord, and boldness. What is interesting to note, however, is the truth unearthed in the opening portion of Proverbs 28:1, "The wicked flees when no one is pursuing." The Hebrew term for wicked (עָרָשׁ *rasa*) can be translated as in the wrong, guilty, or having an unrighteous cause. When a person has an unrighteous cause, they will flee or become victim to the proverbial choke factor when pressure is applied. Williams (2011) asserts that:

> The brain also can work to sabotage performance in ways. Pressure-filled situations can deplete a part of the brain's processing power known as working memory, which is critical to many everyday activities. Beilock contends as a result of her research that working memory helps people perform at their best in physical, intellectual and applied situations including business. This working memory is located in the prefrontal cortex that serves as a limited temporary storage for information needed to complete immediate tasks. Very talented and able people have larger working memories, but this is where the problem arises. When **anxiety** or **fear** [emphasis mine] creeps in, the working memory becomes overtaxed, and you lose the brain power to succeed.[20]

From military battlefield to corporate boardroom, a cursory examination of history will reveal that the choke factor has undermined the performance of many different entities. Perhaps the preoccupation with personal guilt, or the lack of a righteous cause, was the contributing factor for 306 British soldiers to desert the fight in World War I, who were subsequently executed for being cowards?[21] Maybe it was the internalized wrongness of the cowardly leaders of Enron that led their team to defraud Americans of millions of dollars? Additionally, is the lack of a righteous cause a plausible explanation for the indifference of thousands of bystanders who passively witness wrong and do nothing, every day? To conclude this litany of reasonable inquiries, one can infer that the choke factor was the logic behind President George Washington's belief that, "with inexpressible concern that cowardice was a crime of all others, the most infamous in a Soldier, the most injurious to an Army, and the last to be forgiven; inasmuch as it

---

[20]Williams, Ray. 2011. "Why we choke under pressure and what to do about it." *Psychology Today*. June 24. Accessed September 24, 2017. https://www.psychologytoday.com/blog/wired-success/201107/why-we-choke-under-pressure-and-what-do-about-it

[21]Walsh, Chris. 2014. *Cowardice: A Brief History*. Princeton, NJ: Princeton University Press. p. 14.

may, and often does happen, that the Cowardice of a single officer may prove the destruction of the whole Army."[22] The choke factor is such a hazardous act that Washington believed it to be the cancer of an entire organization. Maybe this is the very reason this vice is the leading one to experience the second death of fire and brimstone, as described in Revelation 21:8?

ANTIDOTES FOR FEAR

The question now becomes, "What are the cures for fear?" To offer a reasonable and biblical answer to this question, a sermon given by Martin Luther King Jr., called *Antidotes for Fear* will be analyzed. As this American led the national discussion on reconciliation, without a security detail or bodyguards, he was faced daily with threats in an attempt to derail his righteous cause of freedom for all people. As King navigated his own personal anxieties, this dreamer made a case for four antidotes to overcome fear. Before outlining his argument, King made a key distinction between normal and abnormal fears by noting that, "Normal fear motivates us to improve our individual and collective welfare; abnormal fear constantly poisons and distorts our inner lives. Our problem is not to be rid of fear but rather to harness and master it."[23]

In light of the above, the first prescription that King offers to help a leader is to unflinchingly face our fears and to honestly ask ourselves why we are afraid.

If this advice is embraced, one will find that premise of most dread is rooted in misinformation that has blossomed into a phobia. It is akin to a child who heard the sound in a dark room without understanding that the noise was a dog leaving the area. Because they never understood or was given the tools to process through tough questions, that child's imagination ran amuck, and an abnormal fear was born. To this end, the ability for a person to ridicule our mindset is the master cure for fear and anxiety.[24]

---

[22]Washington, George. 1775. "The Papers of George Washington digital edition." *General Orders.* July 7. Accessed September 24, 2017. http://rotunda.upress.virginia.edu/founders/GEWN-03-01-02-0040

[23]Martin Luther King Jr. 1963. *A Gift of Love: Sermons from Strength to Love and Other Preachings.* Boston: Beacon Press. p. 117.

[24]Ibid.

King contends that the second cure to fear is the supreme virtue of courage. More specifically, King states,

> Courage and cowardice are antithetical. Courage is an inner resolution to go forward despite obstacles and frightening situations; cowardice is a submissive surrender to circumstances. Courage breeds creative self-affirmation; cowardice produces destructive self-abnegation. Courage faces fear and thereby masters it; cowardice represses fear and is thereby mastered by it. Courageous men never lose the zest for living even though their life situation is zestless; cowardly men, overwhelmed by the uncertainties of life, lose the will to live. We must constantly build dikes of courage to hold back the flood of fear.[25]

It is the practice of daily building dikes of courage that can strengthen one's inner resolve. That is, doing "acts of small courage," such as speaking up for the voiceless, opening the door for the elderly, or picking up the piece of paper everyone "chooses not to see," which can prepare one when the giants of life emerge.

The third antidote for fear is love and 1 John 4:18 states that "There is no fear in love; but perfect love cast out fear: because fear hath torment. He that fears is not made perfect in love." While reflecting on this passage, King points out that, "The kind of love which led Christ to a cross and kept Paul un-embittered amid the angry torrents of persecution is not soft, anemic, and sentimental. Such love confronts evil without flinching and shows in our popular parlance an infinite capacity 'to take it.' Such love overcomes the world even from a rough-hewn cross against the skyline.[26]" To this end, one's ability to walk in Godly love could very well be the difference between cowardice and courage, particularly when the moment is demanding.

The final remedy of King's for mastering fear is through faith. At the heart of this assertion is a matter of belief. That is, where will one ultimately place one's hope and confidence? Will you believe the report affiliated with the negative, which can lead you to being a coward? Or will you trust and act in a manner that believes the essences of the promises of the Lord? One such passage can be found in Matthew 10:28, "And do not fear those who kill the body but cannot kill the soul. But rather fear Him who is able to destroy both soul and body in hell." In other words, the

[25] Ibid. p. 119.
[26] Ibid. p. 122.

only being a person should ultimately fear, or reverence is God. For such reverence will only infuse within the soul of a leader the courage to engage and accomplish tasks that transcend our abilities.

BOARDROOM BOLDNESS CHATS

As it pertains to Edmund Burke's assertion of "All that is required for evil to triumph is for good people to do nothing," what were some of the possible reasons for the silence in King David's Royal court?

Martin Luther King Jr., made a case for just and unjust laws. Do you agree with this argument? Be sure to discuss your logic in detail.

Zimbardo makes a compelling case that climate (i.e., apple barrels) can corrupt the citizens (i.e., apples) of an organization. Take a position for or against and explain.

Of the seven contributing variables that Zimbardo contends leads to evil, which are the more problematic?

What is meant by the seven factors of a spiritual organization, and which factor is the most important?

What does it mean to be righteous and how is this displayed at the tactical, operational and strategic levels?

What are the four antidotes for fear, and which one resonates the most with you? Explain.

CHAPTER 3

You Have the Right to Remain Silent. Or Do You?

THE FIRST BOARDROOM LANGUAGE

When it comes down to impacting an organization, an analysis of the literature seems to suggest that an influencer has an array of languages at their deposal to help mitigate wrong and to discern between Martin Luther King Jr.'s notion of just and unjust laws. To recap, just decrees uplift the human personality, whereas an unjust directive degrades the human spirit. As illustrated in Figure 3.1, the first linguistic choice is to "shut up." But before a leader invokes the option to instantaneously and silently obey orders, one has an obligation first to discern the essence of the directive. This was Joab's dilemma. The second son of Zeruiah, David's sister, and brother of Abishai and Asahel (1 Chr. 2:16) had an interesting background that made him loyal. He earned the title of chief commander of the royal forces because he was the first to defeat the Jebusites, the people David's soul hated (2 Sam 5:8). Joab was highly decorated and accomplished in this role of defending the interests of the nation. He led the charge in restoring portions of the city of David (1 Chr 11:8), he brought justice on the Arameans for their act of humiliation on David's ambassadors (2 Sam 10:1–14), and secured the city of Rabbah for the king (2 Sam 11:1). However, Joab was also used by David to murder Uriah the Hittite, Bathsheba's husband. Perhaps it was this experience that convicted Joab and caused him to scrutinize the morality of further orders, as opposed to acting in blind obedience?

© The Author(s) 2018
M. A. Buford, *Bold Followership*, Christian Faith Perspectives in Leadership and Business, https://doi.org/10.1007/978-3-319-74530-5_3

43

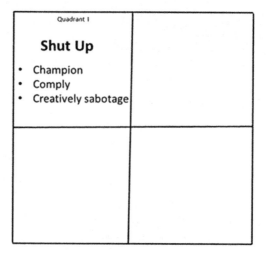

Fig. 3.1 Boardroom boldness language model—quadrant I

LESSONS FROM URIAH THE HITTITE

The literature is relatively silent with regards to understanding the life of Uriah. We do know, however, that he was first a Hittite. According to Smith and Cornwall, the descendants of Heth were viewed as an annoyance.[1] Although this view may have been true collectively, it did not necessarily apply to the person of Uriah, due to his status as a hero and a mighty warrior in David's army (1 Chr 11:41). One can also observe the character and discipline of Uriah when the king summoned him back under the false pretext of learning about the siege of the Ammonites at Rabbah. In an attempt to cover up his transgression David insisted on Uriah going home. When this ethical warrior refused, David was reminded of the strategic imperative that right is more powerful than might. Observe the lesson in progress:

> "…Why did you not go down to your house?"[11] And Uriah said to David, "The ark and Israel and Judah are dwelling in tents, and my lord Joab and the servants of my lord are encamped in the open fields. Shall I then go to

---

[1] Smith, S., & Cornwall, J. (1998). In *The Exhaustive Dictionary of Bible Names*. North Brunswick, NJ: Bridge-Logos, p. 104.

my house to eat and drink, and to lie with my wife? *As* you live, and *as* your soul lives I will not do this thing." (2 Sa 11:10–11)

Uriah stood on principle by sleeping close to the king, even after attempts to get him intoxicated. Such values propelled Uriah to sleep on a hard floor with honor rather than go home to comfort and therefore violate a code of conduct. As a result, David instructed Uriah to return to the fight with a handwritten note for Joab that was undoubtedly sealed by the king's signet ring. What did this executive order direct the commander of the royal army to do? "Set Uriah in the forefront of the hottest battle, and retreat from him, that he may be struck down and die (2 Sa 11:15)."

AN ETHICAL PAUSE

As Joab quietly recited the order delivered by the hand of Uriah, he must have experienced an internal struggle like no other. Nevertheless, after Joab carried out this unethical order, he learned that not only was Uriah murdered but so were an unspecified number of other servants of David whom he knew personally (2 Sam 11:17). This haunting reality apparently caused him a moral injury that would forever shape his future decisions. Being scarred by the Uriah incident, Joab seemingly observed three things. First, he witnessed good *people* get murdered. Second, he observed the *process* in which it occurred (i.e., set Uriah in the forefront of the hottest battle, and retreat from him, that he may be struck down and die). Third, he slowly read the *policy* of the king that made it so. These same three aspects would later help Joab to better manage the ethical space between an order and its execution. For, in the case of Uriah the Hittite, Joab the commander was morally defeated because he did not adequately manage the ethical pause.

Viktor Frankl reportedly once said that "Between stimulus and response there is a space. In that space is our power to choose our response. In our response lies our growth and our freedom." To utilize this logic in the context of the battlefield or the boardroom, one can say that between order and execution there is a space. Although such a space may very well be limited, there still is a gap, as depicted in Fig. 3.2. In this book this break is referred to as an ethical pause, the seconds, minutes, or brief time span a follower has in which to determine if a directive is morally fit to execute. Moreover, as Joab's dilemma will indicate, a leader should first wrestle internally with a set of questions to determine its moral fitness.

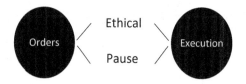

Fig. 3.2 The ethical pause model

Such questions should revolve around the people, process, and policy, then these very questions should be respectfully presented to the author of the order. To return to a previous point, observe how Joab better managed the ethical pause in the face of this second account of king-think.

> ³And Joab answered, "May the LORD make His people a hundred times more than they are. But, my lord the king, are they not all my lord's servants? Why then does my lord require this thing? Why should he be a cause of guilt in Israel?"⁴ Nevertheless, the king's word prevailed against Joab. (1 Ch 21:3–4)

Notice the question with regards to the people, "My lord the king, are they not all my lord's servants?" This simple yet profound inquiry was perhaps Joab's proactive yet subtle way of protecting an undetermined number of people. The process question pondered, "Why then does my lord require this thing (i.e., reducing God's people to a number)? The policy question wondered, "Why should he (i.e., the King's executive decision) be a cause of guilt in Israel?" Such queries seemingly align with the sentiments of Maxwell when he asserted that, "Questions unlock and open doors that otherwise remain closed."² If this is true, then those within the metaphorical royal court of the king have an obligation to first unlock and open doors with questions. This simple yet important gesture may very well be the off ramp that allows our respective leaders to exit safely the prison doors of king-think.

SILENT MORAL INJURY

It has been said that in the end, we will not remember the words of our enemies but the silence of our friends. Such silence, however, comes at a high price that often goes unnoticed. The cost can be described as "the

---

²Maxwell, John C. 2014. *Good Leaders Ask Great Questions*. Orange, CA: Hachette Book Group, p. 8.

pain that results from damage to a person's moral foundation."[3] Gibbsons-Nebb explains moral injury by suggesting that, "damage to the inner person occurs when there is a failure to hold oneself or others to account."[4] Dripchat and Jamshid suggest that moral injury has an array of symptoms, which include:

> difficulties with social functioning, spiritual or ethical problems, cognitive and emotional symptoms, and occupational performance. More specifically, the symptoms of moral injury include the following: negative changes in ethical attitudes and behaviors; changes in and losses of spirituality; problems with guilt, shame, and the ability to forgive; anhedonia, dysphoria, and a reduced trust in others; aggressive and self-harm behaviors; and poor self-care.[5]

In other words, when a wrong is initiated, like that of King David on Uriah, the wounds cut deeper than the eye can behold. In addition to the loss of innocent life, one can argue that due to Joab's inactions, he acquired a silent moral injury that slowly chipped away at his soul and his overall productivity. When such a wound is allowed to fester without acknowledgment and treatment, it can ultimately lead to destruction.

CHAMPION THE ORDER

The question now becomes, "What happens if a leader answers the questions affiliated with the ethical pause (i.e., people, process, and policy) with the silent treatment—as David did to Joab—and their flawed decision stands?" This is the quandary of the twenty-first-century workforce, and often a follower tragically decides to speak the first language of quadrant I—*shut up and champion the order*. Championing the order in the scenario of this book essentially means not only numbering the people swiftly but creating a more robust system to count future generations, all for the sake of the king's ego. This component of the boardroom model can be likened to a warrior aggressively committing acts of genocide on an

---

[3] Gibbons-Nebb, Thomas. 2015. "Haunted by their decisions at war." *Washington Post* March 6. Accessed September 30, 2017. https://www.washingtonpost.com/opinions/haunted-by-their-decisions-in-war/2015/03/06/db1cc404-c129-11e4-9271-610273846239_story.html?utm_term=.70391da6fc6c

[4] Ibid.

[5] Dripchak, Valerie L., and Jamshid A. Marvasti. 2016. "Moral Injury in War Veterans: Seeking Invisible Wounds." *Social Work Today.* September/October. Accessed September 30, 2017. http://www.socialworktoday.com/archive/092116p18.shtml

48 M. A. BUFORD

entire village, when the initial order was to wrongfully murder one person. If a follower elects to employ this course of action, they should be advised that the justification of "trying to please the boss" will not resolve the guilt, the moral injury, or the crime.

A historical case of shut up and champion the order is the My Lai massacre. On March 16, 1968, a company of 100 soldiers was sent into the village of My Lai in South Vietnam with orders to suppress guerrilla forces. The intelligence report indicated that many of the opposition forces were living among the population and that once the American forces arrived, most locals would be out of the village engaged in the market. The company commander in charge was Captain Ernest Medina who, contextually speaking, had the reputation of being a firm but fair leader with the men, and was also known to impose a provocatively high standard, even though he referred to his men as the death dealers.[6] Moreover, Medina taught the men to leave behind an ace of spades whenever a Viet Cong was killed.

Another contributing personality to the mission was Lieutenant William Calley, who oversaw a platoon. It should be noted that Calley was not held in high regard with his men and the psychiatrist who evaluated him indicated that he was, "a rather passive young man harboring a deep-seated sense of inadequacy, insecurity, and inferiority."[7] Calley and the other men of Charlie Company listened intently the night before the mission as Medina translated the order to suppress the opposition in My Lai. According to a series of interviews conducted by Laser Film Corp in 1970 with war veterans, the overall impression of the operation's brief was to kill and destroy everything. This imprint was a logical inference for the listeners, particularly since: 60 percent of Americans believed the war in Vietnam was not right; it was difficult to engage the opposition; and the men wanted revenge for the loss of life of popular soldiers.[8]

Charlie Company embarked upon helicopters and was inserted in the designated landing zone. Charged with emotion, flawed intelligence, and a mindset of being death dealers, Charlie Company immediately began to destroy everything that moved. This killing spree became more disturbing as time went on, as epitomized by the raping and killing of women, the slaughtering of infants and of the elderly. Perhaps the most horrific tipping

[6]Lindsay, Drew. 2012. "Something Dark and Bloody: What happen at My Lai?" *HistoryNet*. August 7. Accessed September 30, 2017. http://www.historynet.com/something-dark-and-bloody-what-happened-at-my-lai.htm

[7]Ibid.

[8]McMahon, Robert J. 2003. *Major Problems in the History of the Vietnam War: Documents and Essays*. Boston: Houghton Mifflin. p. 504.

YOU HAVE THE RIGHT TO REMAIN SILENT. OR DO YOU? 49

point of the entire incident was the mass murder of some 80 innocent villagers. In the testimony of Paul Meadlo a rifleman who helped gather a group of men, women, children, and babies in the center of the village:

> Lieutenant Calley came over and said, "You know what to do with them, don't you?" And I said, "Yes." And he left and came back about 10 minutes later, and said, "How come you ain't killed them yet?" And I told him that I didn't think he wanted us to kill them, that he just wanted us to guard them. He said, "No, I want them dead." So he started shooting them. And he told me to start shooting. I poured about four clips into them."[9]

When the dust settled, some 500 inhabitants of My Lai had been murdered at the hands of US Forces. Although this was the reality, the narrative that was pushed up the chain of command, and ultimately out to the nation, was "The combat assault went like clockwork & US Troops Surround Reds, Kill 128."[10] However, the truth was eventually revealed to the world in a package of appalling photos and earth-shaking journalism. This form of boardroom language, which will be explored in Chap. 5, educated leaders on the brutal facts and demonstrated how Lieutenant Calley essentially championed an order of suppressing the opposition to being the principle catalyst of destruction. Additionally, it should be noted that many of the parties to this massacre not only ended innocent lives, but their own souls were also forever damaged from the wounds of moral injury.

As one processes the ramifications of championing the order, through the lens of My Lai, one can discover three indicators that should caution organizations in today's context. First, elements of Zimbardo's psychology of evil (see Chap. 2) were at play. Second, the perpetuators of the carnage remained haunted the rest of their natural lives and nursed their moral injuries due to their actions. The third indicator revolved around the passive nature and the overall sense of the inadequacy of Calley. Stated differently, when a follower's natural propensity is for timidity, and they harbor seeds of insecurity, that person may have a deep psychological desire to receive validation from authority. This mindset of being a man pleaser (Eph 6:6–8), unfortunately, may very well be the principle cause of keeping a person from doing the right thing.

---

[9] Lindsay, Drew. 2012. "Something Dark and Bloody: What happen at My Lai?" *HistoryNet*. August 7. Accessed September 30, 2017. http://www.historynet.com/something-dark-and-bloody-what-happened-at-my-lai.htm

[10] Ibid.

COMPLY WITH THE ORDER

In a similar vein as championing the directive, an influencer can elect to comply. The inference of this boardroom dialect is that a follower will salute and obey, but at the bare minimum speed. Stated slightly differently, a follower sees and understands that a particular order lacks moral clarity. Due to this reality, their ethical pause is overruled by logical justification. Their reasoning may revolve around a belief, as in King David's royal court, "That certainly the Lord's anointed leader would not march us into a harmful predicament." Additionally, the realities affiliated with earning a salary, or not wanting to be viewed as a troublemaker, may keep the average follower's head down as they endeavor to fly under the proverbial radar. Unfortunately, this very mindset can be problematic and even life altering.

An example of the just following orders verbiage is the response of some of the employees of Enron. At one point Enron was the seventh largest company in the world and reported an excess of 101 billion dollars in 2000. This corporation employed some 20,000 and was constantly crowned with the title of being *Fortune 500 Magazine*'s "America's Most Innovative Company". But behind the curtains, personalities pulling the levers epitomized king-think. The culture established by the likes of Jeffery Skilling and Ken Lay was relentless, to say the least. The climate was undergirded by a performance review committee (PRC) that annually ranked the workforce on a scale of 1–5. The top percentage were rewarded, while the bottom 15 percent were placed in a lower bracket that ultimately led to termination.[11] This practice, coupled with the aggressive narrative of greed being good, as well as deceptive policies, placed most Enron employees in a difficult position. When a follower dared to question the practices or a decision made by executives, they were either ignored or fired.[12] For many an honest Enron worker, who needed a paycheck, and who depended on the corporation to make a living or to support sick loved ones, just following orders seemed to be the only option.

Another toxic case of the just following orders variety is the Jonestown massacre. In 1956 Jim Jones started a church named the Peoples Temple. The overarching vision of this church was to build a community that focused on helping people in need. Contextually speaking, such a message

---

[11] Gibney, A. 2005. *Enron: The smartest guys in the room [motion picture]*. United States: Magnolia Pictures.

[12] Martin, Jason. 2017. "Organizational Culture and How Enron Did it Wrong." *Linkedin*. February 23. Accessed October 7, 2017. https://www.linkedin.com/pulse/organizational-culture-how-enron-did-wrong-jason-martin-mba

resonated with hundreds of people during a divisive moment in American culture that resulted in a radically diverse church, demographically. As the congregation grew, so did the ambition of the church's founder. As a result, the Peoples Temple decided to move from Indianapolis, Indiana, to Redwood Valley, California, in 1966. This relocation would prove to be an infamous and pivotal point in history. In California Jones quickly made a name for himself. He was perceived as a champion of the powerless. This graduate of education from Butler University in Indianapolis adopted several children from different ethnic backgrounds and had a track record of helping marginalized people overcome setbacks.[13] Moreover, Jones quickly became a political powerbroker in California, due to the estimated 20,000 members who faithfully followed his ideology.[14]

Such momentum energized Jones to cast a vision for the congregation to relocate to Guyana. After securing approval to lease land from the Guyanese government in 1973, an advance party from the Peoples Temple moved there to begin building the notorious Jonestown. Although the project was not set to be completed for several years, Jones expedited the moving process when he learned that an unfavorable article about his practices was about to be published by a local editor. This article, which will be discussed in more detail in Chap. 5, became the catalyst for Jones, and hundreds of his most dedicated followers, to suddenly move to Guyana the day before the publication hit the stands on August 1, 1977. The sudden move to an uncompleted project created problems, discomfort, and waves of complaints from the congregation. Such grievances made it back to the States on November 18, 1978. As a result, "U.S. Representative Leo Ryan from San Mateo, California heard reports of bad things happening in Jonestown; thus, he decided to go to Jonestown and find out for himself what was going on. He took along his adviser, an NBC film crew, and a group of concerned relatives of Peoples Temple members."[15]

At first glance, everything appeared fine from the point of view of the Representative. That perception quickly changed, however, when someone passed a note to the news crew during a dinner reception that he or she wanted to leave. This revelation prompted the delegation to offer anyone at Jonestown who was there against their will a chance to fly back to

[13] Kilduff, Marshall, and Phil Tracy. August 1, 1977. "Inside Peoples Temple." *New West* 30–38.

[14] Ibid.

[15] Rosenberg, Jennifer. 2017. "The Jonestown Massacre." *ThoughtCo*. August 3. Accessed October 8, 2017. https://www.thoughtco.com/the-jonestown-massacre-1779385

52   M. A. BUFORD

the States with them. This gesture would prove to be the tripwire for Jones to order an attack on the Representative and his associates. After they were murdered, Jones,

> told them that because of the attack, Jonestown was not safe. Jones was sure that the U.S. government would react strongly to the attack on Ryan's group. '[W]hen they start parachuting out of the air, they'll shoot some of our innocent babies,' Jones told them. Jones told his congregation that the only way out was to commit the 'revolutionary act' of suicide. One woman spoke up against the idea, but after Jones offered reasons why there was no hope in other options, the crowd spoke out against her.[16]

To this end, some 1000 people drank grape-flavored Flavor-Aid laced with cyanide and valium. Although reports indicated that many complied with the order willingly, others were forced to obey with weapons pointed at them with the intent to kill.

A TALE OF TWO COMPLIANT ORGANIZATIONS

Serendipitously, the cases outlined in this section appear to have exploited the dark side of social psychology. To illustrate, Zimbardo argued, in unpublished research, that it was plausible that Jones was largely influenced by the work of George Orwell. More specifically, Zimbardo suggests that Orwell's fictional book *1984*, outlined a scheme to maximize mindless compliance, particularly in the face of wrong. As depicted in Table 3.1, such a system was also used by the leadership of Enron. The first tactic revolved around the narrative that, "Big Brother is watching

Table 3.1   A tale of two complying organizations

	Leadership	Org size	Big brother	Self-incrimination	Destructive model	Distortion	End state
Enron	Jeffery Skilling and Ken Lay	20 K	PRC	PRC	Shredding	Mark-to-market accounting	Bankrupt
Peoples Temple	Jim Jones	20 K	PA system	Family meetings	Suicide drill	Newspeak	Mass suicide

[16] Ibid.

you." In the scenario of Jones, the people were required to spy on one another as an act of loyalty. Additionally, in Guyana, Jones would utilize frequent messages from loudspeakers to reinforce the persona that he was constantly observing.[17] Enron, in a similar fashion, used the platform of the PRC to command loyalty and to breed a larger than life imagining in the ideology of the followers.

The second tool that both entities utilized was self-incrimination. Jones imposed this tool by requiring followers to write statements about their fears and mistakes. In the event that Jones was disobeyed, they would be humiliated at what was referred as "family meetings" with everybody in attendance.[18] In a similar vein, Enron's methodology to command a fierce allegiance was again the PRC. To reiterate a previous point, the bottom 15 percent of the Enron workforce was on thin ice due to their "rank and yank" climate. This environment cultivated abuse, condoned back stabbing, and looked away when the top performers dehumanized the bottom percentile.

The third mechanism invoked to guarantee compliance with the masses were suicide drills. Zimbardo suggests that in *1984* "Orwell's main character said that the proper thing was to kill yourself before they get you in a threat of war."[19] This suggestion was seemingly central to the indoctrination of the followers of Jones. To illustrate, Jones would constantly rehearse suicide drills with the expectation of following through if the compound were ever to be threatened. Although there is no evidence that this practice was taught at Enron, they did, however, employ companies like Shredco to destroy some 7000 pounds of documents an hour when their company was on the verge of collapse.[20] The regrettable logic behind this gesture was to ensure that the veil of secrecy would be sealed forever.

The final element that breeds mindless compliance is the distortion of people's perceptions. In the case of Jones, his cult personality made it difficult to discern between words and reality. Again, Zimbardo contends that Jones required "his followers to give him thanks for good food and work, yet the

---

[17] Dittmann, Melissa. 2003. "Lessons from Jonestown." *American Psychological Association.* November. Accessed October 8, 2017. www.apa.org/monitor/nov03/jonestown.aspx

[18] Ibid.

[19] Ibid.

[20] Ross, Brain. 2002. "Enron Destroyed Documents by the Truckload." *ABC News.* Janurary 29. Accessed October 9, 2017. abcnews.go.com/WNT/story?id=130518&page=1

54 M. A. BUFORD

people were starving and working six and half days a week."[21] This practice, known as "newspeak" as lifted from *1984*, was designed to diminish the range of thought. Enron's version of newspeak was predicated on a concept known as mark-to-market accounting. This pathway, indigenous to the fiscal world, allows one to measure the value of a security based on the current market value as opposed to the book value. This loophole, unfortunately, was aggressively exploited by Enron executives and thereby blurred the lines between fact and fiction.

CREATIVELY SABOTAGE THE ORDER

In light of the hypnotic realities affiliated with followers caught in the above quandaries, the question becomes, "Is there a better option than merely complying with immoral orders?" Joab's action, as outlined in 1 Chronicles 21:4–6, illuminates a feasible answer and offers the final element of the *shut up* boardroom language. Consider the creative actions of this bold follower

> Therefore Joab departed and went throughout all Israel and came to Jerusalem.[5] Then Joab gave the sum of the number of the people to David. All Israel *had* one million one hundred thousand men who drew the sword, and Judah *had* four hundred and seventy thousand men who drew the sword.[6] But he did not count Levi and Benjamin among them, for the king's word was abominable to Joab.

As depicted in the above verses, Joab reported to the king that 1,570,000 men could draw the sword in Israel and Judah. Joab did not, however, number Levi and Benjamin because he viewed the order as repulsive. However, the question becomes, why leave Levi and Benjamin out of the equation? Was it because the Levites were the keeper of the Tabernacle of Testimony and that the Benjaminites were strategically located near the presence of God (i.e., the Tabernacle of Testimony)? One can only speculate, but it is for certain that Joab tried to creatively sabotage the order by not giving a full report and by doing it with disdain. Unfortunately, such an endeavor was not enough to exempt him or the

---

[21] Dittmann, Melissa. 2003. "Lessons from Jonestown." *American Psychological Association*. November. Accessed October 8, 2017. www.apa.org/monitor/nov03/jonestown.aspx

entire nation from what was to come, but it was an innovative gesture to stand up to a corrupt practice.

An additional historical example of creatively sabotaging an immoral directive is the underground railroad. The personalities affiliated with this network demonstrated a keen ability to challenge and innovatively undermine an immoral practice. To recap, there are two types of laws—just and unjust. "A just law is a human-made code that squares with the moral law or the law of God. An unjust law is a code that is out of harmony with the moral law. To put in terms of St. Thomas Aquinas: An unjust law is a human law that is not rooted in eternal law and natural law. Any law that uplifts human personality is just. A law that degrades human personality is unjust."[22] The American way, and the best practices of the land, authorized an unjust system known as slavery. This free labor, particularly in the South from 1780 to 1862, made plantation owners very wealthy and powerful, at the expense of the bodies and souls of African Americans. If one were to place a collective price tag on the value of their work, experts suggest it would be the equivalent of two trillion to four trillion dollars today.[23]

Due to the inhuman and un-American treatment of slaves, a network of bold followers organized a method that allowed the oppressed to escape to freedom. This journey to the North and Canada was not the effort of a single personality. On the contrary, the underground railroad was a string of locations (i.e., churches, homes, safe places, and businesses) that provided refuge to those who exercised the courage to pursue what was affectionally referred to as the Promised Land. The stations, as they were called, were run by both white and black people who understood the dangers associated with being indifferent. Although there is insufficient evidence to give credit to the originator of this network, the record indicates that the Society of Quakers played a tremendous part—in 1786 George Washington complained how this faith community helped one of his runaway slaves.[24]

To fully appreciate the courage and the creative ability to sabotage the American system of slavery, one must try to understand life through the

---

[22] Martin Luther King Jr. 1963. "Letter from Birmingham Jail." *The Estate of Martin Luther King Jr.* April 16. Accessed March 14, 2017. http://kingencyclopedia.stanford.edu/kingweb/popular.requests/frequentdocs/birmingham.pdf

[23] Conley, Dalton. 2003. "The Cost of Slavery." *The New York Times.* February 15. Accessed October 14, 2017. http://www.nytimes.com/2003/02/15/opinion/the-cost-of-slavery.html

[24] PBS. 2016. "The Underground Railroad." *Judgment Day part 4 PBS.* Accessed October 14, 2017. https://www.pbs.org/wgbh/aia/part4/4p2944.html

lens of a slave in the eighteenth century. Imagine you and your beloved family being chained and put on display, like a herd of cattle, to be sold to a potential buyer. You hear words that you do not understand because it is not your native language, but you manage to comprehend that you have just been sold at the going rate of $150. Fear, trauma, and pain overwhelm you as you watch your family desperately scream as they are snatched from you and sold to other buyers. Once you make it back to your new "home," you quickly learn that disobedience to any order from your master means public lashes on the back, more dehumanization, or being lynched. Moreover, you have no means to live, and the laws of the land are on the side of slave owners.

The above scenario was the geo-political reality of slaves—no rights, no respect, and they had no legal power. What they did have, however, was a boldness that permeated from God, like that of a lion. It was this lion-like boldness that propelled slaves to escape, and it was a network of countless others who enjoyed the freedom to accept that they too had a moral responsibility to disobey unjust laws. But perhaps the face of the underground railroad and the chief engineer of creatively sabotaging the slavery order was Harriet Tubman. This courageous woman is given credit for making 19 trips on the underground railroad and escorting over 300 slaves to freedom, all while bounties were posted for her arrest or death. Although this boardroom language did not immediately halt the American slavery system, it can be argued that it was a righteous first step to challenge the flawed mental model of a nation.

In like manner, so was the gesture of Joab with David's order. In a sense, Joab was creating his version of the underground railroad by releasing the Levites and Benjaminites from the tyranny of king-think. It is worth noting at this point that both Joab and Tubman engaged in this boardroom language with the proper spirit. In other words, these two exemplars of this boardroom dialect demonstrated four traits that others in this quadrant did not display. First, in these incidents, they both stood on the premise that right makes might. This righteous position seemingly empowered them not to champion or comply sheepishly with an unjust order. Second, they inserted an innovative and just solution into degrading practices. It is interesting to note that scholars contend that creativity has a process. Such a progression includes the starting point of preparation. From a starting point a leader endeavors to understand the problem and gather all the relevant information.[25] Next, an influencer embarks

[25] McShane, Steven L., and MaryAnn Glinow. 2013. *Organizational Behavior.* New York: McGraw-Hill Irwin. p. 208.

upon the incubation phase. During this period, one begins to reflect, and the information simmers on a nonconscious level, where divergent thinking occurs.[26] After a season of cultivating of information, having flashes of illumination, a divine revelation springs forth from a spiritual perspective. This sudden awareness, however, may emerge in an incomplete or vague form, but an idea is conceived.[27] Once the idea surfaces, this new-found thought enters the verification mode, where detailed logic undergirds the fresh awareness.

The third common denominator that these exemplars of creative sabotaging showcased were heroic courage. Zimbardo suggests that four key elements must be present to constitute a person being brave. The act

(a) must be engaged in voluntarily; (b) it must involve a risk or potential sacrifice, such as the threat of death, an immediate threat to physical integrity, a long-term threat to health, or the potential for serious degradation of one's quality of life; (c) it must be conducted in service to one or more other people or community as a whole; and (d) it must be without secondary, extrinsic gain anticipated at the time of the act.[28]

In light of this fearlessness gage, one can reasonably say that both Joab and Tubman not only met but exceeded the standard. Finally, they executed their strategic plan, to quietly undermine an immoral practice, without incident, for the sake of the nation. There deliberations were never about them but ultimately for the team. To coin it slightly differently, such quiet acts of valor were saying through their action that we are better than this self-centered order.

BOARDROOM BOLDNESS CHATS

The Improvised Explosive Device (IED) Case

You are a noncommissioned officer within an infantry battalion. Your company commander has recently informed your team on deployment that yet another soldier was killed by an IED planted near a local village. This casualty will be the seventh this month, and each time another member of the team dies, your appetite for vengeance soars. While on patrol

---

[26] Ibid.

[27] Ibid.

[28] Zimbardo, Philip G. 2007. *The Lucifer Effect: Understanding How Good People Turn Evil*. New York: Random House. p. 466.

Fig. 3.3 The spectrum of "shut up" boardroom language

one evening, you notice four local villagers all of a sudden drop something and run into a house about 100 yards away. Things did not seem right so you, the most senior ranking leader, and ten other soldiers chase them into the house where things quickly get out of control. They do not speak your language, but they are yelling at the top of their voice. Your senior ranking leader shouts out an order, "Let's take care them, the same way they took care of our fallen brothers!"

1. While reflecting on the IED case, have a discussion on whether or not an ethical pause is warranted. If you decide that there is no time for an ethical pause, please explain your logic. If you decide there is time, please clearly explore the *people, process and policy* elements of your conversation.
2. In which category would you place the senior ranking leader's order—just or unjust? Please discuss in detail.
3. What is a moral injury? Please discuss the best practice to mitigate and treat it.
4. As you reflect upon the IED case, please apply each element of the spectrum of the *shut up* boardroom language see depicted in Fig. 3.3. Within your discussion, please explore the ramifications of each course of action.
5. Have a conversation on Zimbardo's four criteria for heroic courage and which traits can be infused in the boardroom.

CHAPTER 4

Faithful Are the Wounds of a Friend

The Second Boardroom Language

Joab's ethical questions about people, process and policy seem to have taken root in the king's consciousness for 2 Samuel 24:10 indicates, "And David's heart condemned him after he had numbered the people." This reawakening within the king set the stage for the second boardroom language to be delineated—*speak in*. Speaking in can be defined as a follower's ability to utilize truth as a tool to transform both a leader's paradigm and their toxic behavior. Moreover, the premise of *speaking in* assumes that a follower has accessibility to their metaphorical king, usually due to their position at court.

In All of Your Getting

If an influencer has been trusted with proximity to a leader, it is imperative they embrace the counsel of Solomon, as recorded in Proverbs 4:7–8, "Wisdom *is* the principal thing; *Therefore* get wisdom. And in all your getting, get understanding. Exalt her, and she will promote you; She will bring you honor, when you embrace her." With regard to the boardroom language of *speaking in*, it would be a prudent gesture to understand the leader's preferred method of communication, which will increase the probability of the message being heard and proactively mitigate the loss of time. According to the emerging research of Mark Murphy, there are four

© The Author(s) 2018
M. A. Buford, *Bold Followership*, Christian Faith Perspectives in Leadership and Business, https://doi.org/10.1007/978-3-319-74530-5_4

methods of transmitting messages that leaders typically employ within an organization. They include:

The **Analytical Communicator** likes hard data, real numbers, and tends to be suspicious of people who are not in command of the facts and data. They typically like very specific language and dislike vague language.
The **Intuitive Communicator** likes the big picture, avoids getting bogged down in details, and cuts right to the chase. They do not need to hear things in perfect linear order but prefer instead a broad overview that lets them easily skip right to the end point.
The **Functional Communicator** likes process, detail, timelines and well-thought-out plans. They like to communicate things in a step-by-step fashion, so nothing gets missed.
The **Personal Communicator** values emotional language and connection and uses that as their mode of discovering what others are really thinking. They find value in assessing not just how people think, but how they feel.[1]

A thorough understanding of the bosses' means of communication is the prelude to speaking in and is a fundamental virtue of bold followership. A bold follower goes the extra mile for an excellent leader who provides a legal and moral direction. This same follower has a righteous mandate to stand up to a flawed leader in the name of organizational health. Such a stance, to emphasise the point, is predicated on John 8:21, "you will know the truth, and the truth will set you free." The operative word in this passage is *know*—γινώσκω. The Greek term can be translated as to make acquaintance of, to learn, or find out. Thus, in this context, when a follower puts in the effort to learn about a leader's preferred method of communicating, then freedom will spring forth. That is, barriers that have the potential to undermine the sending and receiving of messages (i.e., presenting data to a personal communicator or details to a bottom line personality) will be removed, and the follower can focus on navigating the ensuing insights.

Speaking in with a Parable

The first methodology to speak in the life of a leader is a parable as depicted in Fig. 4.1. Copenhaver contends that "A parable is a weapon of weakness... A parable, however, can get past the defenses of our own behavior

---

[1] Murphy, Mark. 2016. "My Boss And I Have Different Communication Styles, And It's Destroying Our Relationship." *Forbes*. April 24. Accessed October 16, 2017. https://www.

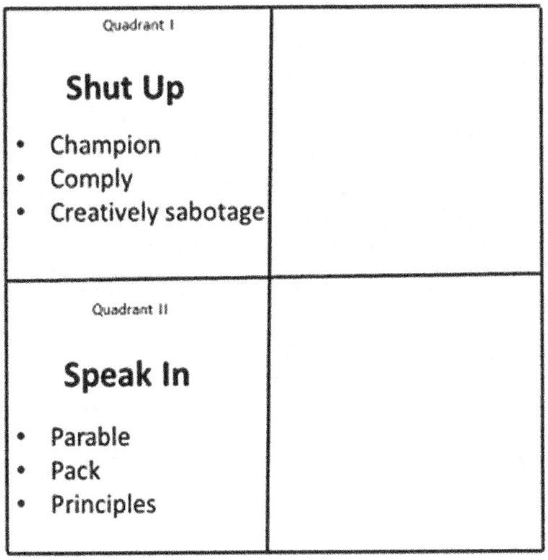

Quadrant I **Shut Up** • Champion • Comply • Creatively sabotage	
Quadrant II **Speak In** • Parable • Pack • Principles	

Fig. 4.1 Boardroom boldness language model—quadrant II

and reach the inner court where there is agreement about what is right and what is wrong…"[2] Such a weapon was utilized on David when his defenses were still up after the murder of Uriah. In 2 Samuel 12:1–7 we are told that Nathan entered the presence of the king in a respectful and dignified manner and painted a picture of a tale of two men. One was rich, and the other was poor. The rich man had an abundance of flocks whereas the poor man only had one lamb whom he loved. The rich man, explains the parable, unjustly took the poor man's lamb for selfish purposes. After presenting the details of the parable, David became furious at the man because he did not have mercy. To which, Nathan announced that the king was that man! As this story shows, parables can be an effective tool of correction when defenses are still up, but in this case, the narcissistic behavior of king-think had already subsided. Thus, such a technique would not neccessarily be advantageous in this scenario, but the following parable forms may be applicable.

forbes.com/sites/markmurphy/2016/04/24/my-boss-and-i-have-different-communication-styles-and-its-destroying-our-relationship/#70fdd36e38cc

[2] Copenhaver, Martin B. "He spoke in parables." *Christian Century*, July 13–20, 1994: 681.

The Parable of Data

The first form of a parable that a follower can employ to *speak in* the life of a leader is with data, which is when the sentiments of W. Edward Demming ring true, "In God we trust, but everyone else must bring data." Demming was a leading voice in the total quality management movement and an advocate of fixing systems to move the needle on production. In other words, painting an empirical picture of the organization can resonate for an analytical leader. Due to their propensity to be suspicious of assertions not grounded in data, this numeric parable can help a follower get past the defenses of flawed behavior and reach the inner court of consciousness. Such numbers, however, should never be purposefully skewed but should be presented in a valid, reliable, and ethical manner.

The Parable of BLUF

The bottom line up front (BLUF) approach is the second parable form. The BLUF tactic, which is primarily indigenous to the military, is essentially a practice of placing the recommended course of action at the beginning as opposed to the end of a conversation. This mechanism seeks to quickly answer the five W's: who, what, where, when and why.[3] By swiftly and accurately answering the five W's, it acknowledges that an executive is operating on a tight timeline and that it is critical to provide recommendations up front. This pathway, if delivered correctly, is ideal for the intuitive boss who values the big picture. Thus, if this form of parable is delivered with precision, the mindset of an executive could be transformed.

The Parable of a Manual

The third parable at the disposal of a follower is that of a manual. A book of instructions for operating a machine, learning a subject, or running a team is the language of the functional leader. This personality lives in the details of an issue, and the articulator of this parable form must be clear about the procedures. It would behoove a follower, in this example, to research the company's polices and synthesize the boss's intent in a logical direction. This pathway can proactively answer questions, eradicate any

---

[3] Sehgal, Kabir. 2016. "How to Write Email with Military Precision." *Harvard Business Review.* November 22. Accessed October 21, 2017. https://hbr.org/2016/11/how-to-write-email-with-military-precision

FAITHFUL ARE THE WOUNDS OF A FRIEND   63

perception of incompetence from the leader's perspective, and allow the truth locked within a manual to penetrate the heart of an influencer.

THE PARABLE OF CORPORATE STORYTELLING

The final parable form a follower can invoke to foster transformation is corporate storytelling. As in Nathan's conversation with David, this approach embraces company narrative to persuade. Denning contends that there are four types of story a follower can embrace.

First is the tale of a new business model, in which an influencer helps the sponsors or managers to see how the business will work once the change is undertaken.[4] This form of a story is predicated on the theory of business, either in the now or in the near future. Denning suggests that when embracing this narrative form a follower should endeavor to answer questions like, "Who is the customer? What does the customer value? How do we win (i.e., accomplish the mission)? What is the underlying logic that shows how we can deliver value to customers?"[5] President John F. Kennedy's *We Choose to Go to the Moon* speech is a stellar example of this model. JKF argued:

We set sail on this new sea because there is new knowledge to be gained, and new rights to be won, and they must be won and used for the progress of all people. For space science, like nuclear science and all technology, has no conscience of its own. Whether it will become a force for good or ill depends on man, and only if the United States occupies a position of pre-eminence can we help decide whether this new ocean will be a sea of peace or a new terrifying theater of war. I do not say that we should or will go unprotected against the hostile misuse of space any more than we go unprotected against the hostile use of land or sea, but I do say that space can be explored and mastered without feeding the fires of war, without repeating the mistakes that man has made in extending his writ around this globe of ours. There is no strife, no prejudice, no national conflict in outer space as yet. Its hazards are hostile to us all. Its conquest deserves the best of all mankind, and its opportunity for peaceful cooperation may never come again. But why, some say, the Moon? Why choose this as our goal? And they may well ask, why climb the highest mountain? Why, 35 years ago, fly the Atlantic? Why does Rice play Texas? *We choose to go to the Moon!* …We choose to go to the Moon in this decade and do the other things, *not* because they are easy, *but because*

[4]Denning, Steve. 2011. "The Four Stories You Need To Lead Deep Organizational Change." *Forbes Magazine.* July 25. Accessed October 22, 2017. https://www.forbes.com/sites/stevedenning/2011/07/25/the-four-stories-you-need-to-lead-deep-organizational-change/#acaba1953b29
[5]Ibid.

they are hard; because *that goal* will serve to organize and measure the best of our energies and skills, because *that challenge* is one that we are willing to accept, one we are unwilling to postpone, and *one we intend to win*[6]

It can be argued that the above section of JFK's speech was the driving factor in Apollo 11's landing on the Moon on July 20, 1969. Although this is a macro level example, it can be reduced to a micro aspect and be applied to smaller organizations.

A criticism of the new business model is that it can be perceived as too abstract and those on the receiving end may be inclined to marginalize this delivery pathway. To this end, the second type of corporate storytelling— the burning platform story—may resonate. The intent of the burning platform, contends Denning, is to explain "why the way of operating in the past that was so successful is no longer successful and is leading to disaster."[7] This rhetorical appeal is important and should be grounded in the theory of the other side of innovation; the story should specifically caution against not falling victim to traps that are physical (i.e., investing in old systems), psychological (i.e., depending on past glories) or strategic (i.e., focusing on today's marketplace).[8]

The problem with this approach is that one can seem alarmist or pessimistic. Although the message may be factual, it may not be well received due to its tone. Hence, the third approach that can be employed is the springboard story, which is "is a story about the past—something that's already happened and because it has already happened, it is very believable. Because it is positive, it tends to spark action."[9] To restate this point biblically and in a slightly different manner, one should be guided by the wisdom found in Ecclesiastes 1:9, "That which has been *is* what will be, that which *is* done is what will be done, And *there is* nothing new under

---

[6] Kennedy, John F. 1962. *Rice University Speech*. Rice University, Houston. September 1.

[7] Denning, Steve. 2011. "The Four Stories You Need To Lead Deep Organizational Change." *Forbes Magazine*. July 25. Accessed October 22, 2017. https://www.forbes.com/sites/stevedenning/2011/07/25/the-four-stories-you-need-to-lead-deep-organizational-change/#acaba1953b29

[8] Newman, Rick. 2010. "10 Great Companies That Lost Their Edge." *U.S. News*. August 19. Accessed October 23, 2017. https://money.usnews.com/money/blogs/flowchart/2010/08/19/10-great-companies-that-lost-their-edge

[9] Denning, Steve. 2011. "The Four Stories You Need To Lead Deep Organizational Change ." *Forbes Magazine*. July 25. Accessed October 22, 2017. https://www.forbes.com/sites/stevedenning/2011/07/25/the-four-stories-you-need-to-lead-deep-organizational-change/#acaba1953b29

the sun." As one looks for "that which has been done" in an organization, offering historical models may be the catalyst to spur modification. The final corporate story can invoke the past as an influencer paints a vivid picture of the unspoken attitudes and assumptions that exist in a corporation. Such assumptions, however, have become so ingrained that they are no longer seen. This reality becomes problematic to production, particularly when behaviors undermine the mission. Karl Weick's sentiments ring true when he asks, "how can I know what I think, until I see what I say."[10] This story type takes the corporate thoughts of an organization and paints a relevant picture to help a leader see the impacts of past practices and the current emotions of the people. In the end, a picture is indeed worth a thousand words, particularly for the personal communicator.

SPEAKING IN WITH STRATEGIC PACK

The second system of speaking in the life of a leader is with the assistance of a strategic pack, alliance, or coalition. This pathway could indeed be a game changer, particularly for the leader who places a high premium on loyalty and an even higher subconscious value on having "yes people" around them. Such people are placed very close to the leader and are often rewarded with high ranking positions in the royal court. Such positions of privilege grant the followers access to the king's ear and by mobilizing these key personalities to communicate the same message to a leader suffering from king-think could remedy a flawed organizational decision. To illustrate this pathway, consider this course of action that successfully unfolded in the latter days of David's life of, as recorded in 1 Kings 1:1–14:

Now King David was old, advanced in years; and they put covers on him, but he could not get warm.[2] Therefore his servants said to him, "Let a young woman, a virgin, be sought for our lord the king, and let her stand before the king, and let her care for him; and let her lie in your bosom, that our lord the king may be warm."[3] So they sought for a lovely young woman throughout all the territory of Israel, and found Abishag the Shunammite, and brought her to the king.[4] The young woman *was* very lovely; and she cared for the king, and served him; but the king did not know her.[5] Then Adonijah the son of Haggith exalted himself, saying, "I will be king"; and he prepared for himself chariots and horsemen, and fifty men to run before

[10]Weick, Karl. 1979. *The Social Psychology of Organizing*. New York: McGraw-Hill.

him.[6] (And his father had not rebuked him at any time by saying, "Why have you done so?" He *was* also very good-looking. *His mother* had borne him after Absalom.)[7] Then he conferred with Joab the son of Zeruiah and with Abiathar the priest, and they followed and helped Adonijah.[8] But Zadok the priest, Benaiah the son of Jehoiada, Nathan the prophet, Shimei, Rei, and the mighty men who *belonged* to David were not with Adonijah.[9] And Adonijah sacrificed sheep and oxen and fattened cattle by the stone of Zoheleth, which *is* by En Rogel; he also invited all his brothers, the king's sons, and all the men of Judah, the king's servants.[10] But he did not invite Nathan the prophet, Benaiah, the mighty men, or Solomon his brother.[11] So Nathan spoke to Bathsheba the mother of Solomon, saying, "Have you not heard that Adonijah the son of Haggith has become king, and David our lord does not know *it*?[12] Come, please, let me now give you advice, that you may save your own life and the life of your son Solomon.[13] Go immediately to King David and say to him, 'Did you not, my lord, O king, swear to your maidservant, saying, "Assuredly your son Solomon shall reign after me, and he shall sit on my throne"? Why then has Adonijah become king?'[14] Then, while you are still talking there with the king, I also will come in after you and confirm your words."

Within this passage, David was near to the end of his life, and Adonijah, son of Haggith, had made moves to appoint himself the new king of Israel. David's indifference about the manner (i.e. David had not rebuked him at any time by saying, "Why have you done so?") signaled to the nation that a new policy had been formulated—Adonijah will be the new king. In an endeavor to suppress this power play, Nathan created a strategic pack with Queen Bathsheba to speak in David's ear about the plot and remind him that Solomon was the preferred choice. This unlikely alliance persuaded David to muster up the strength to outmaneuver Adonijah and have Solomon declared as his successor.

Yulk elaborates on the utilization of packs, alliances, or coalitions. More specifically, this scholar contends that followers should "mention the names of others who endorse a proposal when asking the person to support it. Get others to explain to the person why they support a proposed activity or change. Bring someone along for support when meeting with the person to make a request or proposal. Get others to explain to the person why they support a proposed activity or change."[11]

[11] Yulk, Gary. 2010. *Leadership in Organizations*. New Jersey: Prentice Hall. p. 182.

A powerful example of such guidance was on display at the assembly of the First Continental Congress. Under British rule of the 13 American colonies, the tyranny of the king of Great Britain would prove to be overwhelming as the crown exercised authority with a firm fist from 1607 to 1776. However, as the enlightenment period took root and bold followers were being divinely positioned, the grip of the throne began to falter. With a litany of illegal and immoral acts imposed upon the colonies, those who fled oppression in hopes of freedom found themselves at a defining moment. Such a moment emerged upon parliament's approval to bail out the East India Company. This corporation was a pivotal cog in the economic machinery of the British government, for it generated £400,000 per year and owed the government £1,300,000 in 1773.[12] Due to fiscal necessity, the government devised a strategy to reinvigorate the firm and to keep the economy strong with yet another tax on the colonies, without representation.

Upon receiving notification of their intent and knowledge of three tea ships (i.e., the Dartmouth, the Eleanor, and the Beavor) being in port, colonial sympathizers—the sons of liberty—dressed up as Mohawk Indians and creatively sabotaged the government's plan by emptying 342 tea chests into the sea. This act, now famously referred to as the Boston Tea Party, infuriated the crown, and a measure was devised to starve the entire city into submission.[13] Moreover, the British insisted that the port remain closed until three conditions were met:

- The city apologized for the actions of the Boston Mutineers
- The East India Company had been reimbursed for the tea that had been destroyed
- The perpetrators of the crime had been presented for punishment.[14]

Once the news of the crown's latest action made its way through the colonies, one bold follower decided to build a strategic pack. On May 11, 1774, Samuel Adams called a meeting and made the recommendation to renew an old boycott of British goods. A byproduct of the gathering was a plan that read,

---

[12] Thompson, James C. 2010. *The Dubious Achievement of the First Continental Congress.* Alexandria, VA: Commonwealth Books. Kindle Loc. 628.

[13] Ibid.

[14] Ibid.

68   M. A. BUFORD

It is the opinion of this town, that if the other colonies come into a joint resolution to stop all importation from Great-Britain and the West Indies, till the act for blocking up this harbor be repealed, the same will prove the salvation of North-America and her liberties. On the other hand, if they continue their exports and imports, there is a high reason to fear that fraud, power, and the most odious oppression, will rise triumphant over justice, right, social happiness, and freedom. And moreover, that this vote be transmitted by the moderator, to all our sister colonies, in the name and behalf of this town.[15]

The essence of this document was used to build a Solemn League or Covenant that called on every colonist to unite. Not only did this pack successfully resist the new demands of the crown but it also served as the key ingredient for a declaration of independence.

SPEAKING IN WITH PRINCIPLES

The third method to *speak in* is on principles. Principles, or standing on a set of values, when engaging a leader can be an equalizing factor. Chaleff explains this by asserting that, "followers usually cannot match up to a leader's external qualities, such as the trappings of formal power, and must find equal footing on intellectual, moral or spiritual ground"[16] A biblical example of speaking in with principles for the nation of Israel would be Gad, whose name can be translated as *good fortune*, was a relatively unknown yet powerful presence. When David was fleeing from King Saul and hiding in the cave of Adullam, it was Gad who gave him the principled counsel to go to Judah (1 Sam. 22:5). When the occasion called for an accurate and reliable chronicling of the life of David, Gad was named as one of the three to record history (1 Chr 29:29). Moreover, when the fate of a nation was hanging in the balance, it was the best practice found in 1 Chronicles 21:9–12— that prevailed.

Then the LORD spoke to Gad, David's seer, saying,[10] "Go and tell David, saying, 'Thus says the LORD: "I offer you three *things;* choose one of them for yourself, that I may do *it* to you."'"[11] So Gad came to David and said to him, "Thus says the LORD: 'Choose for yourself,[12] either three years of fam-

[15]Cohen, Lester H. 1990. *The History of the American Revolution.* Indianapolis: Liberty Fund.
[16]Chaleff, Ira. 1995. *The Courageous Follower.* San Franciso: Berrett-Koehler Publishers, Inc. p. 26.

ine, or three months to be defeated by your foes with the sword of your enemies overtaking *you*, or else for three days the sword of the LORD—the plague in the land, with the angel of the LORD destroying throughout all the territory of Israel.' Now consider what answer I should take back to Him who sent me."

HISTORICAL TRUST

Four principles can be abstracted from Gad's methodology of *speaking in* the life of a leader as depicted in Fig. 4.2. The foundational concept revolves around historical trust, which can be defined as the positive and established expectations one person has toward another in situations involving risk.[17] To recap, Gad more than likely established trust by encouraging and advising David long before he was a king hiding in a cave. In 1 Samuel 22:5, David fled from Saul and requested refuge in Moab until he learned what the Lord would do for him (1 Sam 23). While there, the Lord sent Gad to provide a firm command to depart. Scholars suggest that such a directive was stated as a categorical prohibition, using a clause structure parallel to that employed in the Ten Commandments (cf. Exod 20:4–5, 12–17). The reason for the strong wording is simple: the Torah prohibited the establishment of friendly treaties with Moabites (cf. Deut 23:2–6). As a true prophet of the Lord, Gad's duty was to help others understand and heed the Torah. If David established such a treaty with the king of Moab, he would violate the Torah and so risk bringing judgment on himself and all who were with him.[18]

Fig. 4.2 The aspects of speaking in

[17] McShane, Steven L., and MaryAnn V. Glinow. 2013. *Organizational Behavior: Emerging Knowledge. Global Reality.* New York: McGraw-Hill Irwin., Loc 3986.
[18] Bergen, R. D. (1996). *1, 2 Samuel* (Vol. 7, pp. 225–226). Nashville: Broadman & Holman Publishers.

70 M. A. BUFORD

It should be noted that the counsel Gad gave David was risky because such an action could have been perceived as a treasonous act since Saul was still the reigning king who had a track record of murdering those who dared to assist David. This feat of putting his life on the line to help a young leader to survive the Saul's deadly grip must have elevated David's confidence in this prophet. This point is key, particularly in a culture that seems to applaud coat tail riding and being an opportunistic user of others. Without proven historical trust being the foundation of a relationship, one's ability to engage a leader may very well be over long before it begins.

SPIRITUALITY

The second driving factor that can be gleaned from Gad is spirituality, which equipped him with clarity of thought during times of ambiguity. Such clarity provided the prophet with the right message, at the right time, and gave him the right motive—to serve the son of Jesse in the same way he had done before David had power. Additionally, this seer's spirituality was his ultimate fuel for boardroom boldness, as Proverbs 28:1 reminds the reader, "the righteous are as bold as a lion." In other words, the closer one gets to walking in truth and living with a purpose, the more powerful the voice. It is this form of spirituality (i.e., being bold as a lion) that seemingly empowered Gad to use the third element of *speaking in*—straight talk.

STRAIGHT TALK

As 1 Chronicles 21:11 indicates, "So Gad came to David and said to him, 'Thus says the Lord'." What is interesting to note is what is not outlined in this brief text—pleasantries. Gad did not waste time catching up, breaking the ice, or sugarcoating. On the contrary, this adviser's historical trust allowed him to press through the royal court and bypass any gatekeeper to get to David. Once he made it to his destination, he talked straight. Covey describes this term best when he wrote that influencers should, "Be honest. Tell the Truth. Let people know where you stand. Use simple language. Call things what they are. Demonstrate integrity. Don't manipulate people or distort facts. Don't spin the truth. Don't leave false impressions."[19] It is this bold yet tactful showcasing of love that seemingly opened the door of David's heart to receive the next aspect of speaking in—courses of action.

[19]Covey, Steven. 2006. *The Speed of Trust*. New York: Free Press. p. 143.

COURSES OF ACTION

The final principle that can be learned from Gad is the way he clearly outlined courses of action for David to select. Although neither of the options was appealing, they were nonetheless clear, proportional, and factual. Consider David's options, "Choose for yourself,[12] either three years of famine, or three months to be defeated by your foes with the sword of your enemies overtaking *you*, or else for three days the sword of the LORD—the plague in the land, with the angel of the LORD destroying throughout all the territory of Israel." The average boardroom member may be reluctant to present such hard courses of action out of fear. However, such individuals should take note that their obligation is to advise boldly and the leader's job is to decide ethically. In David's case, he decided for himself when he invoked king-think. Influencers should also be reminded of the truth located in Proverbs 27:6, "Faithful are the wounds of a friend." If this is true, then a possible inference is that one cannot be a friend if one is unwilling to *speak in*, even if it is painful.

BOARDROOM BOLDNESS CHATS

The 1985 New Coke Case

You are a member of the executive board of Coca-Cola in 1985. In an endeavor to keep the competitive edge, a study was commissioned to understand how the public would respond to a New Coke. A New York Time's report captured both the essence of the study and the decision of the executives, "When the Coca-Cola Company introduced a reformulated version of the world's best-selling soft drink on April 23, it was well aware that it might alienate some faithful Coke drinkers. The company, however, expected that alienation to fade. It was completely unprepared for how it would spread and deepen in the two months following the debut of the new Coke."

Fig. 4.3   The spectrum of "speak in" boardroom language

1. While reflecting on the 1985 New Coke case, have a discussion on the best method to understand the top executives' preferred style of communication.
2. Have a discussion on the meaning and the possible application of a parable in this particular case to help reformulate a flawed executive decision. Within your discussion, role play the various forms of parable in this scenario.
3. Have a discussion on the meaning and the possible application of utilizing a pack in this particular case to help reformulate a flawed executive decision. Within your discussion, role play how one could possibly build a workplace "Solemn League or Covenant."
4. Have a discussion on the meaning and the possible application of standing on principles in this particular case to help reformulate a flawed executive decision. Within your dialog be sure to make a case for the most important component of *speaking in* with principles as depicted in Fig. 4.3.
5. Have a conversation on whether a hybrid of the *speaking in* would help or hinder the advisement role.

CHAPTER 5

A Prescription for Organizational Dis-eases

THE THIRD BOARDROOM LANGUAGE

[14]So the LORD sent a plague upon Israel, and seventy thousand men of Israel fell. [15]And God sent an angel to Jerusalem to destroy it. As he was destroying, the LORD looked and relented of the disaster, and said to the angel who was destroying, "It is enough; now restrain your hand." And the angel of the LORD stood by the threshing floor of Ornan the Jebusite. (1 Ch 21:14—15)

ORGANIZATIONAL DIS-EASES

The practices of *shutting up* and *speaking in* the life of a leader, unfortunately, may not produce the level of conviction needed to atone. It may very well take an epidemic or an organizational disease to grab the undivided attention of a leader that is hypnotized with king-think. In the scenario of David, it took 70,000 men dying from plague and the possibility that an entire nation be wiped off the planet to transform one mind. This point deserves illuminating since the actions or inactions of one can impact the lives of thousands and the reader must understand that organizational diseases are only symptoms of sick leadership. In the context of twenty-first-century organization, Lencioni suggests that such diseases may manifest in five distinct ways.[1]

[1]Lencioni, Patrick. 2002. *The Five Dysfunctions of a Team*. San Francisco, CA: Jossey-Bass.

© The Author(s) 2018

M. A. Buford, *Bold Followership*, Christian Faith Perspectives in Leadership and Business, https://doi.org/10.1007/978-3-319-74530-5_5

DISTRUST

The first symptom is a team that lacks trust among themselves. Although all organizations may have pockets of distrust, research suggests that there are four overarching signs of a lack of organizational confidence that need monitoring, the first revolves around excessive control. According to John Bruhn, the author of *Trust and the Health of Organizations*, excessive control limits the input and output of an organization and can undermine justice due to bureaucracy.[2] Organizations that gravitate to this practice are fierce proponents of micromanagement. They believe that intrusive leadership, which is often code for micromanagement, is the best way to control the flow of work, people, and information. Although on the surface this tactic may seem logical to a low-trust organization, in actuality this gesture further erodes confidence.

Such entities do not believe followers can be trusted to do their job. As a result, the quantity of work becomes more important than its quality and new systems are implemented to make workers account, minute by minute, for activities and whereabouts. This rigid form of management may indeed yield busy work and shallow metrics, it will simultaneously minimize risk-taking and corporate innovation, and the art of delegation or empowerment becomes a foreign concept. This is the new reality for low-trust entities, largely due to the distrustful mental model of the leader.

The second sign of a lack of organizational confidence revolves around antagonistic interactions. Again, Bruhn suggests that, "An organization where members spend a great deal of time being cynical, critical, uncivil, blaming, looking over their shoulders, obsessed with their own resources and benefits, take most things personally, volunteer for nothing, and are absent from organizational meetings and social affairs, is a distrustful organization."[3] This parade of antagonistic interactions in a team is perhaps the leading driver of litigation, internal investigations, and silos. This intangible but evident workplace variable will reduce the speed of productivity and create the conditions for an elevation in the number of sick days.

Distancing behavior and communication are the third mark of a distrustful entity. This is when organizational members lack zeal for the mission, constantly criticize goals, socialize outside the team, and distance

---

[2]Bruhn, John G. 2001. *Trust and the Health of Organizations*. New York: Springer Science. [Kindle Loc. 2128.]
[3]Ibid. [Kindle Loc. 2152].

themselves from coworkers.[4] Such behaviors, debatably, are akin to the actions of a spouse on the verge of contemplating a divorce due to unfaithfulness. This self-imposed isolation from the team is, in reality, a defense mechanism to guard against the abuses affiliated with excessive control and an organizational blame game. Moreover, the realities associated with distancing behavior motivate followers to operate at a bare minimum speed. This soft form of dissent not only impacts the bottom line, but also sets the conditions for the fourth indicator of a distrustful organization—the lack of spirit, vitality, and vibrancy.

Bruhn contends that this lack of spirit, vitality, and vibrancy can be felt as an organization limps along. The spark that was once in the eye of the dedicated worker is now glazed over. The gratitude that used to be plastered on the faces of the team has now been replaced with a stoic demeanor. The position that used to be filled almost before it was advertised is now impossible to match with high performers. Because of the lifelessness, the good name of the firm continues to decline as stakeholders quietly distance themselves.

THE CONSEQUENCES OF EXTREME DISTRUST

An extreme and regrettable example of distrust in an organization was displayed by a segment of service members during the Vietnam War. Contextually speaking, the Vietnam War was perhaps one the most controversial engagements in the history of American warfare. The divisiveness was largely hinged on morality as questions were invoked in public such as, "Does America have an ethical case to be there?" "Is the drafting system just?" and "Are the right leaders in charge?" Such questions were habitually left unanswered at the tactical level and, coupled with an eroding confidence in the chain of command, this led to an array of unhealthy outlets. To illustrate, the armed forces reported that desertion levels had increased, riots between black and white service members were the norm, and a growing number of personnel in Vietnam were addicted to narcotics (i.e., in one study 20 percent of 4600 soldiers self-reported.[5])

The most alarming gesture of distrust, arguably, among the service members was a practice known as fragging. This term was made popular after Senator Charles Mathias raised the issue on the Senate floor in 1970

---

[4] Ibid.
[5] Cortright, David. 2005. *Soldiers in Revolt: GI Resistance During the Vietnam War*. Michigan: Haymarket Books.

after the murder of 24-year-old West Point graduate, First Lieutenant Thomas A. Dellwo. Fragging, explained the Senator, refers to the use of a fragmentation grenade to kill or do bodily harm in other than a combat situation.[6] Before things escalated to that point, however, all parties would endeavor to *work it out*. *Working it out* first started in Vietnam, where the practice was normalized. The procedure was simple. If a unit or man refused to advance or take an order, everybody—including officers and sergeants—would sit down and talk. During the conversation, a safer route or alternative job was agreed upon. Officers and sergeants in Vietnam who refused to participate in such talks became prime candidates for being fragged.[7] Unfortunately, an estimated 1017 fragging incidents occurred in Vietnam, which resulted in 86 fatalities and 714 injuries.[8] Presumably many of these tragic incidents could have been mitigated if a trust factor between leader and follower had been present.

THE FEAR OF CONFLICT

The second major symptom of organizational dis-ease is the fear of conflict. One can argue that there are two sides to the conflict coin. On one is the inability to handle conflict, as when organizational citizens cease to adhere to or understand the counsel of Proverbs 27:17, "As iron sharpens iron; so one person sharpens another." The inference of this text is that the sharpening process will produce sparks, generated as two distinct pieces of iron are intentionally rubbed together to produce a sharper tool. Unfortunately, due to the lack of trust, members are reluctant to engage in the process in the which one party perceives that his or her interests are being opposed or negatively affected by another party.[9] This hesitancy ultimately undermines both person and organization as key team members withdraw from the sharpening process. The result becomes a lack of learning, progressing, and growth as a team.

[6]Brush, Peter. 2010. "The Hard Truth About Fragging." *Historynet*. July 28. Accessed October 31, 2017. www.historynet.com/the-hard-truth-about-fragging.htm/2

[7]Ayres, B Drummond. 1971. *Army Is Shaken by Crisis In Morale and Discipline*. New York: The New York Times.

[8]Gabriel, Richard A., and Paul L. Savage. 1978. *Crisis in Command*. New York: Hill & Wang. p. 183.

[9]McShane, Steven L., and MaryAnn Glinow. 2013. *Organizational Behavior*. New York: McGraw-Hill Irwin. p. 319.

On the other side of the coin is the inability to manage agreement. Harvey (1988) categorises the place where groups embark on an excursion that no member wants to take as the Abilene Paradox. That is, followers, take actions in contradiction to what they want to do and therefore defeat the very purposes they are trying to achieve.[10] Such followers, according to Harvey, manifest six characteristics. First, they individually agree in private about the nature of the situation or problem confronting the organization. Second, they agree on the specific steps needed to address the problem. Third, followers fail to accurately communicate their desires and/or beliefs to one another. Fourth, due to inaccurate communication of one's true beliefs, a false narrative is publicly conveyed to the team. Fifth, due to the public–private disconnect, followers experience frustration, anger, irritation, and overall dissatisfaction with the team. Sixth, if followers do not find the courage, or fail, to employ the proper boardroom language, the cycle will repeat itself, only with greater intensity.[11]

No Skin in the Game

As of a result of distrust and the fear of conflict, it is more than likely that followers will not be inclined to "put skin in the game." This third all-encompassing indicator of organizational dis-ease is a metaphor that describes one's level of commitment and participation in an activity.[12] Tim Schneider suggests that when it comes down to the commitment factor, followers are either interested, involved, or invested. *Interested* followers, to reiterate a previous point, operate at a bare minimum speed. They hardly do what is required and prefer to observe the "game" from the bench, but they are not yet ready to leave the team because they still like the jersey. Followers who fall into this category are essentially ROAD— *retired on active duty.*

---

[10] Harvey, Jerry B. 1988. *The Abilene Paradox and Other Meditations on Management.* San Francisco: Jossey-Base Publishers.

[11] Ibid. p. 16.

[12] Schneider, Tim. 2012. "Leadership Insight: Skin in the game; are you interested or invested." *Evancarmichael.* Accessed November 1, 2017. http://www.evancarmichael.

Followers who are *involved* are not *all in* but, largely because of their Protestant work ethic, they endeavor to make conditions better but their motivation to serve is fading quickly. This reality is predicated in Matthew 9:17, "Nor do they put new wine into old wineskins, or else the wineskin break, the wine is spilled, and the wineskins are ruined. But they put new wine into new wineskins, and both are preserved." In the context of the organization, the unresolved dis-ease has punctured an allegorical hole in their enthusiasm, but they still manage to give proportionate to what remains inside of them. The third type of follower is one who has fully *invested* in the firm as evidenced by their giving of their hands as well as their hearts to the organization. Those who are invested will occasionally send leadership those innovative emails at 3 a.m.[13] due to their level of commitment.

According to Gallup News, only 13 percent of followers worldwide have skin in the game, or are invested.[14] Stated differently, 87 percent of followers are either interested or involved. They are either sleepwalking their way through the day or are actively showcasing their unhappiness with destructive behaviors as the climate slowly chips away at their emotional, physical, and spiritual wellbeing. This truism keeps citizens from investing their talents, time, and treasures to help the team win.

The Lack of Accountability

The fourth sign of a sick team is the lack of accountability. The principles that compose accountability, contends Covey, include responsibility, stewardship, and ownership. The opposite of this behavior is not to take responsibility, to not own up, but rather to say, "It's not my fault." Its counterpoint is to point a finger and blame others, saying, "It's their fault."[15] Stated differently, when the culture is saturated with blaming others for the lack of productivity, and the team's common expression is that it is "not in my job description," the likelihood of accountability being eroded is high. Additionally, offenders of ethical norms increase because members believe that they are above the law and thrive in an anything goes culture.

com/library/tim-schneider/Leadership-insight--Skin-in-the-Game-Are-You-Interested-or-Invested.html

[13] Zak, Paul J. 2017. *Trust Factor.* New York: AMACOM.

[14] Reilly, Robyn. 2014. "Five Ways to Improve Employee Engagement Now." *GALLUP News.* January 7. Accessed November 1, 2017. http://news.gallup.com/businessjournal/166667/five-ways-improve-employee-engagement.aspx

Inattention to Results

The final indication of organizational disease is inattention to results. James 3:14–16 best depicts this ailment by indicating, "But if you have bitter envy and self-seeking in your hearts, do not boast and lie against the truth.[15] This wisdom does not descend from above but *is* earthly, sensual, demonic.[16] For where envy and self-seeking *exist,* confusion and every evil thing *are* there." That is, if one were to conduct an autopsy on the mayhem and maliciousness affiliated with an entity, one would find the core of the issue to be the twin towers called envy and self-seeking. These vices blind followers and ultimately create an urgency to look out for number one at the expense of the team. This unfortunate business practice fosters an ideology of winning by any means necessary, as opposed to winning ethically.

The Cost of Organizational Dis-ease

When organizations begin to display the above symptoms, it not only negatively impacts the bottom line, it can also crush the spirit of the people who make the line possible. In the marketplace, rework and missteps are multiplied. In hospitals and other helping agencies, lives can hang in the balance. In law enforcement, safety gets undermined. In governments, people can die, much like King David's decision causing 70,000 people to perish (I Ch 21:14), which is roughly the entire city of Wilmington, Delaware. Practically speaking, when such dis-eases are on display, a new reality is formulated that requires a response to a deranged gauntlet that has the masses spellbound.

The Gauntlet

In medieval times, when knights and chivalry were the norm, the expression to throw down the gauntlet meant a challenge was being issued. A knight accepted the challenge by picking up the glove or gauntlet, and the appropriate duel would begin. In the situational case of David and likeminded leaders, there are three possible courses of action that citizens can call for to break the spell of king-think. However, to fully

---

[15] Covey, Stephen. 2006. *The Speed of Trust.* New York: FREE PRESS. p. 262.
[16] Howard, Michael, and Peter Paret. 1984. *On War.* New Jersey: Princeton University. p. 131.

80 M. A. BUFORD

understand the logic behind the ensuing boardroom languages, the concept of Clausewitz's trinity should be understood. While reflecting on what it would take to wage a successful military campaign, Clausewitz argued that "The first of these three aspects mainly concern the people; the second the commander and his army; the third the government. The passions that are kindled in war must already be inherent in the people; the scope which the play of courage and talent will enjoy in the realm of probability and chance depends on the particular character of the commander and the army; but the political aims are the business of government alone."[16]

If one were to apply the Clausewitzian trinity to this book, it could be argued that one aspect of this theory is in play. As depicted in Figure 5.2, one facet of the triangle is the government. In this case, the regime (i.e., King David) is the problem and therefore null. The second factor in winning a campaign is the commander. In this instance, Joab, as described in Chap. 3, invoked the tool of creative sabotage to try to un-ring the bell of pandemonium. Unfortunately, the strategic courage, talent, and realm of the probability of Joab were not enough to correct the course. To this end, the last component of the model must be examined—*the people*. The citizens of various organizations are unknowingly draped with enormous untapped power. Michel and Peter Engler echo this point when reflecting on *The Politics of Nonviolent Action*. They state that

> Sharp argued that people have much more power than they typically realize. 'Obedience is at the heart of political power... Rulers or other command systems, despite appearances, [are] dependent on the population's goodwill, decisions, and support.' Sharp's idea was straightforward: if people refuse to cooperate with a regime—if civil servants stop carrying out the functions of the state, if merchants suspend economic activity, if soldiers stop obeying orders—even an entrenched dictator will find himself handicapped. And if popular disobedience is sufficiently widespread and prolonged, no regime can survive.[17]

WHINE

Considering Sharp's observation, the third boardroom language at the disposal of followers is *speaking out*, out as depicted in Fig. 5.1 which has a range of options. Regrettably, due to the disenchantment affiliated with organiza-

[17] Engler, Mark, and Paul Engler. 2016. *This is An Uprising*. New York: Nation Books. p. 90.

Quadrant I **Shut Up** • Champion • Comply • Creatively sabotage	
Quadrant II **Speak In** • Parable • Pack • Principles	**Quadrant III** **Speak Out** • Whine • Whisper • Whistle blow

Fig. 5.1 Boardroom boldness language model—quadrant III

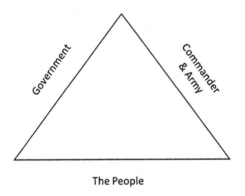

Fig. 5.2 Clausewitz's trinity

tional dis-ease and the unrealized power of the people, the first form of speaking out often leads to *whining*. This negative element of the model is laced with cynicism, unrighteousness, and has no clear agenda, but expresses pent-up frustrations in a public manner. Moreover, those that employ this

82 M. A. BUFORD

method are primarily motivated by anger. Although this passion may indeed be justified in their own eyes, it does not lead to constructive progression. On the contrary, James 1:19–20 maintains, "So then, my beloved brethren, let every man be swift to hear, slow to speak, slow to wrath; for the wrath of man does not produce the righteousness of God." That is, when a person's wrath, ὀργή, informs their actions and decisions, it will never be able to produce the form of righteousness that aligns with godly principles.

A theological example of whining can be found in Numbers 16, which showcases a personality known as Korah making a false charge about their leader, Moses. Verses 2–3 indicate that Korah aroused "two hundred and fifty leaders of the congregation, representatives of the congregation, men of renown.[3] They gathered together against Moses and Aaron, and said to them, '*You take* too much upon yourselves, for all the congregation *is* holy, every one of them, and the LORD *is* among them. Why then do you exalt yourselves above the assembly of the LORD?'"

The problem with such a charge is that it was not true. Moses and Aaron never exalted themselves but had endeavored to follow the Lord's commands as directed. The issue, however, was

> the pride, ambition, and emulation, of great men, have always been the occasion of a great deal of mischief both in churches and states. God by his grace make great men humble, and so give peace in our time, O Lord! Famous men, and men of renown, as these are described to be, were the great sinners of the old world, Gen. 6:4. The fame and renown which they had did not content them; they were high, but would be higher, and thus the famous men became infamous.[18]

Infamous indeed was the outcome of their whining. Because their form of speaking out was not built on truth, but was motivated by vainglory and anger, it resulted in their demise (i.e., verses 31–33 explain that rebellion was swallowed up in the earth).

Another category of whining can be described as riot. A violent collective incident involving 30 or more participants does not usually emerge from a vacuum.[19] Sandra L. Marker's dissertation, *The Ritual of Riots: Discovering A Process Model U.S. Riots*, discovered that several antecedents existed before violence erupted, to include: (1) change in group status; (2) change

[18]Henry, M. (1994). *Matthew Henry's commentary on the whole Bible: complete and unabridged in one volume* (p. 209). Peabody: Hendrickson.

[19]Spilerman, Seymour. 1970. "The causes of Radical Distubances: A Comparsion of Alternative Explanations." *American Sociological Review 36.3*, 627–649.

in life style; (3) change in privilege; (4) change in esteem; and (5) a trigger event. The triggering event, which did not always have a moral imperative, became the catalyst for people to decide to invoke the tool of destruction and speak out without a formal declaration of war. Aggression can be a righteous endeavor when the principles of just war theory are upheld.

Augustine, the Christian architect of the just war theory, offers two guiding principles for a campaign: *Jus Ad Bellum* (the right to go to war); and *Jus In Bello* (the rights in war). Regarding *Jus Ad Bellum*, Augustine asserted that a just or legitimate authority must first declare war. That is, followers not properly elected or selected by a nation cannot formally impose their will upon another agency with force. Second, the cause to go to war must be righteous or just. Third, the act of war should have a proper intention. Finally, the act of war and use of force should be a last resort. It should also be noted that research has demonstrated that non-violent campaigns experience a 50 percent success rate, while violent struggles are victorious 26 percent of the time.[20] Success can be defined as the actual removal of a dictator or flawed leader who perpetuated an evidence-based wrong. Put differently, this form of speaking out has a lower statistical success rate and is further from the scope of this discussion than the ensuing nonviolent boardroom languages.

WHISPERS

A survey of the literature suggests that the second way followers deal with organizational dis-eases is with a whisper, which can be defined as the utilization of informal channels to get a message out to the public. The intent of bringing unethical practices to light is to ultimately suppress, remove, or correct toxic leadership by appealing to the hearts and minds of the masses. Those who pull the lever of whispers seemingly understand that to change the collective minds of the population, one must embrace the 3.5 percent rule, which is an empirical phrase coined by Erica Chenoweth that points to the fact that, "no campaigns failed once they'd achieved the active and sustained participation of just 3.5 percent of the population."[21]

In similar a vein to other boardroom languages, whispers have a spectrum of possibilities. The first form of whispering can be described as *the power of the pen*, which is when a personality or group conducts a writing

[20] Chenoweth, Erica, and Maria J Stephan. 2011. *Why Civil Resistance Works: The Strategic Logic of Nonviolent Conflict*. New York: Columbia University Press. p. 7–9.
[21] Ibid. p. 109.

84   M. A. BUFORD

campaign to expose flawed premises, to educate, and to influence public opinion. A shining example of this are the endeavors of Alexander Hamilton, James Madison, and John Jay. Collectively, these patriots deployed their penmanship in a series of 85 letters known as the Federalist Papers, also referred to as The Federalist, were a sequence of articles that were published in *The Daily Advertiser*, *The New York Packet*, and the *Independent Journal* from October 1787 through August 1788. These articles intended to spark a conversation within the 13 colonies about democracy and liberty in the face of tyranny. Such whispers were written under the pseudonym Publius (Publius Valerius Publicola is credited as the initiator of the Roman Republic) to boldly appeal to the consciousness of the nation. What was the outcome of this boardroom language? A document known as the Constitution of the United States of America was conceived, which reminds the world that, "*We the People of the United States, in Order to form a more perfect Union, establish Justice, insure domestic Tranquility, provide for the common defence, promote the general Welfare, and secure the Blessings of Liberty to ourselves and our Posterity, do ordain and establish this Constitution for the United States of America.*"

It was this form of boardroom language, spoken by the likes of Marshall Kilduff and Phil Tracy, that brought to light the practices of Jim Jones. As alluded to in Chap. 3, members from Jones' congregation began to whisper in the ears of these reporters. Kilduff and Tracy took this knowledge to the masses in an article called *Inside Peoples Temple*. The opening pondered, "Jim Jones is one of the state's most politically potent leaders. But, who is he? And what's going on behind his church's locked doors?"[22] The day before the article was to go public, Jim Jones departed the country, regrettably with those seduced by his spell. Apparently, he did not want to read the August 1, 1977, edition of *New West*, which showcased "Ten who quit the Temple Speak Out." Consider some of the quotes from the article that potentially saved hundreds more lives due to their boldness.

- Elmer and Deanna Mertle of Berkeley: When we first went up [to Redwood]. Jim Jones was a very compassionate person. He taught us to be compassionate to old people, to be tender to the children. But slowly the loving atmosphere gave way to cruelty and physical punishments. The first forms of punishments were mental where they would get up and totally disgrace and humiliate the person in

[22] Kilduff, Marshall, and Phil Tracy. August 1, 1977. "Inside Peoples Temple." *New West* 30–38.

front of the whole congregation... Jim would then come over and put his arm around the person and say, "I realize that you went through a lot, but it was for the cause. Father loves you and you're a stronger person now. I can trust you more now that you've gone through this and accepted the discipline."

- Birdie Marable of Ukiah: One summer she was talked into taking a three-week temple "vacation" through the South and East. Everybody paid $200 to go on the trip... The temple buses were loaded up in San Francisco, and more members were packed aboard in Los Angeles. It was terrible. It was overcrowded. There were people sitting on the floor, in the luggage rack, and sometimes people [were] underneath the compartment where they put everything... I saw how they treated the old people. The bathrooms were frequently stopped up. For food sometimes a cold can of beans was opened and passed around. I decided to leave the church when I got back. I said when I get through telling people about this trip, ain't nobody going to want to go no more. [But] as soon as we arrived back. Jim said... "don't say nothing." She left the church in silence.
- Laura Cornelious of Oakland: The first thing that bothered her was the constant requests for money. After I was in some time it was made known to us that we were supposed to pay 25 percent of our earning... It was called the commitment there were alternatives, like baking cakes to sell at Sunday services—or donating their jewelry. He said that we didn't need the watches—my best watch. He said we didn't need homes—give the home, furs, all of the best things you own.

In the context of the twenty-first century, the power of the pen may indeed include the levering of controversial social media outlets or *the power of the e-pen*. Although the emerging literature seems to suggest there are substantial risks associated with this second form of whispers (i.e., such practices may be not legal but are they moral?), it is, nevertheless, an option for some. There are a plethora of cases that warrant a critical analysis. However, there seem to be two categories of those that embrace leaking through social media. First, there are those who have an ax to grind due to a perceived wrong directed toward them. In this scenario, their motives are not built on righteousness but on reprisal. The other category is those who have a track record of being loyal, responsible, and who positively contribute to the team mission. They are often left alone, regrettably, to navigate the ethical dilemma between right and righteousness. Regardless of where one sits on the topic of the power of the pen, President G. W. Bush's sentiments are applicable when he argued that, "We need an independent media to hold power to account. Power can be very addictive, and it can be corrosive, and it is important for the media to call to account those who abuse their power."

The third form of whispering is *the power of the legal pen*, which is when the principles affiliated with the Whistleblower Protection Act (WPA) apply. The WPA is an American law that protects federal government employees from retaliatory acts for revealing unethical or illegal practices. The majority of organizations have their version of WPA, which allows a follower to report waste, fraud, or abuse to an anonymous 800 hot line or an Investigator General's office. This legal covering allows the concerns of followers to be heard, explored, and handled without fear of being punished for reporting.

BLOW THE WHISTLE

The last mechanism for speaking out or influencing an organization from the outside is by blowing the whistle. The dictionary defines a whistleblower as an informant who exposes wrongdoing within an organization in the hope of stopping it. This person would appeal to someone higher with more power and in a public manner to correct an injustice. Being cognizant of 3.5 principle, and the empirical reality that non-violent campaigns have a 50 percent success rate, while violent struggles only succeed 26 percent of the time,[23] embracing the best practices of Martin Luther King Jr. may be a logical organizational step. In his famous 1963 *Letter from Birmingham Jail*, King outlines the what and the why of this boardroom language. He writes,

> I am in Birmingham because injustice is here. Just as the prophets of the eighth century B.C. left their villages and carried their 'thus saith the Lord' far beyond the boundaries of their home towns, and just as the Apostle Paul left his village of Tarsus and carried the gospel of Jesus Christ to the far corners of the Greco-Roman world, so am I compelled to carry the gospel of freedom beyond my own home town. Like Paul, I must constantly respond to the Macedonian call for aid... In any nonviolent campaign there are four basic steps: (1) collection of facts to determine whether injustices are alive; (2) negotiation; (3) self-purification; and (4) direct action...

[23] Chenoweth, Erica, and Maria J Stephan. 2011. *Why Civil Resistance Works: The Strategic Logic of Nonviolent Conflict*. New York: Columbia University Press. p. 7–9.

The above guidance, coupled with strategic planning and the power of the media, made a movement of Project C (confront), which was the code name of the Birmingham engagement. Project C intended to demonstrate and magnify the ills of racial injustice peacefully. Their analysis predicted that the public safety commissioner, Eugene "Bull" Connor, would arrest in masses and employ force to disband the protest. Bull Connor's decision to use water hoses on the marchers and dogs on the youth would prove to be the defining moment of the campaign. As the media broadcast dogs biting children and water flinging people around, most Americans became appalled. A month after the event, "President John F. Kennedy gave a major televised address announcing that he would put forward civil rights legislation. The events in Birmingham and elsewhere has so increased cries for equality that no city or state or legislative body can prudently choose to ignore them."[24] Disenfranchised, nonviolent whistleblowers were able to change the legal minds of an entire nation.

Would Project C work in another context? Let us briefly apply this question to the United States navy. According to Tomlinson, the navy experienced an increase of incidents affiliated with oxygen poisoning in the 30-year-old T-45 Goshawk. In 2012 there were 11.86 T-45 physiological episodes (involving approximately 12 pilots), whereas in 2016 the figure had climbed to 46.97 episodes (involving approximately 47 pilots) per 100 Km flight hours.[25] These incidents led to histotoxic hypoxia, the medical term associated with a disorientating disorder that can put pilots' lives at risk, as well as those of civilians on the ground.[26] Considering this reality, approximately 100 US navy instructor pilots employed Project C and refused to fly. This action stimulated a conversation with the senior leaders and grabbed the attention of lawmakers. Senator Joni Ernst went to investigate personally and was allowed to experience what the pilots had experienced. In her own words, "It was a terrifying experience for me, I'll be honest about that. They walked us through what symptoms we might have as the oxygen was reduced and it was just like textbook. My face got hot and flush; my fingers started tingling, then got numb; my legs started

[24] Engler, Mark, and Paul Engler. 2016. *This is An Uprising*. New York: Nation Books. p. 107.

[25] Tomlinson, Lucas. 2017. "Navy Instructor pilots refusing to fly over safety concerns; Pence's son affected." *Fox News Politics*. April 4. Accessed November 9, 2017. http://www.foxnews.com/politics/2017/04/04/navy-instructor-pilots-refusing-to-fly-over-safety-concerns-pences-son-affected.html

[26] Ibid.

tingling; it was hard to concentrate—very hard to concentrate."[27] Although the problem has not been 100 percent ratified at the time of writing, the naval version of Project C has set the conditions for transformation as Congress has demanded regular updates on the matter.

SIGNS AND WONDERS

The above tactics are tools available to a follower(s) to appeal to the collective consciousness of the people. Even then, such an appeal to the masses may prove to be a challenging endeavor. To this end, the ultimate court, God, may have to intervene in a very public and decisive manner. A survey of the Judeo-Christian scriptures will reveal that God frequently used signs and wonders beyond human effort to correct unrighteousness. As depicted in 1 Chronicles 21:14–15, the Lord used the tool of a plague to try and disrupt the hardened heart of David. Exodus 5–14 recounts how God employed various signs and wonders to get Pharaoh to let the people go. History will suggest that the hand of the Lord has indeed intervened at various places and times to turn the heart of the king like the waters of a river (Proverbs 21:1). In the end, whether by the divine hand of God or the tool of nonviolent means, the end state is the same—repentance.

BOARDROOM BOLDNESS CHATS

The 401(k) Ethical Case

You are a follower in an organization that at one point was named as one of the top ten companies in the nation. That reputation, however, quickly diminished when the new CEO took charge. Within four years, the company went from first to worst. The new norm has become low morale, distrust, and a daily decline in productivity. You have actionable knowledge that the CEO is tapping into the company's 401(k) plan to fund his lavish lifestyle. A team of fellow followers who are not close to the CEO have decided to do something since mid- and upper-management seem to be looking out only for themselves or may be a part of the unethical practice.

---

[27] Larter, David B. 2017. "Lawmaker demands regular updates on combating pilot oxygen deprivation." *DefenseNews*. November 8. Accessed November 9, 2017. https://www.defensenews.com/naval/2017/11/07/lawmaker-demands-regular-updates-from-the-navy-on-combating-hypoxia/

Fig. 5.3 The spectrum of "speak in" boardroom language

1. While reflecting on the 401(k) ethical case, have a discussion on the symptoms of organizational dis-ease and which ones may be in operation.
2. Have a discussion on the meaning and the possible application of Clausewitz's trinity in this case. Within your discussion, be sure to think through the implications when the leadership and government are silent.
3. Have a discussion on the meaning and the possible application of *whining* as depicted in Fig. 5.3 in this particular case to help reformulate a flawed executive decision. Within your discussion, role play how this may or may not help.
4. Have a discussion on the meaning and the possible application of how the various forms of *whispering* to help reformulate a flawed executive decision. Within your dialog be sure to make a case for the most critical component of whispering—pen, e-pen or legal pen.
5. Have a conversation on employing Project C in a twenty-first-century workforce.

CHAPTER 6

Walking Away to Win the Day

Then David lifted his eyes and saw the angel of the LORD standing between earth and heaven, having in his hand a drawn sword stretched out over Jerusalem. So David and the elders, clothed in sackcloth, fell on their faces.[17] And David said to God, "Was it not I who commanded the people to be numbered? I am the one who has sinned and done evil indeed; but these sheep, what have they done? Let Your hand, I pray, O LORD my God, be against me and my father's house, but not against Your people that they should be plagued." (1 Ch 21:16-17—)

THE FOURTH BOARDROOM LANGUAGE

History seems to suggest that the only real prescription to break the fever of king-think is a heavy dosage of an organizational shake up, which can be defined as an unusual phenomenon that drastically diminishes the bottom line, morale, overall trust, and confidence in executive leadership; which then sets the conditions for change at the highest level. When the influence of the top leader can no longer move the needle, and the mention of their name generates consternation, it may be time to seriously contemplate another approach.

© The Author(s) 2018
M. A. Buford, *Bold Followership*, Christian Faith Perspectives in Leadership and Business, https://doi.org/10.1007/978-3-319-74530-5_6

Theological Antecedents

From the perspective of the follower, it would be a prudent gesture if several key questions were contemplated before exploring the fourth boardroom language. The first inquiry revolves around the construct known as a person–job fit, which can be defined as the fittingness between the abilities of an individual and the job requirements. Typically, when those two elements align, organizational congruency is the outcome. However, when there is a conflict between the two, the research suggests that a follower has a higher propensity to leave the team.[1] Would the tendency to depart a team multiply when another variable, such as king-think, is placed into the equation? That is, in the face of toxic decision making, does one no longer fit the environment? Theologically speaking, there are an array of passages that can help a follower to navigate the waters of this quandary.

Psalm 127:1 indicates that "Unless the Lord builds the house, they labor in vain who build it; Unless the Lord guards the city, the watchman stays awake in vain." The first principle that can be abstracted from this text is being sure that the Lord's hand was involved in the placement of a follower at a particular house (i.e., organization). As the Psalmist indicates, laboring to construct a house without the Lord's backing will result in a vain outcome. That is, in the context of this book, no degree of boardroom language would come close to resonating if a follower is out of position. Moreover, this misalignment of person–job fit can result in added frustrations when compounded with a narcissistic leader. To this end, it would behoove a follower to intentionally muse upon Psalm 127 as they discern if it was the Lord's perfect or permissive will for them to labor at a certain organization.

The second question that a prudent follower should ponder is, "Have you earned a divorce?" On the surface, this query may seem provocative especially from a Judeo–Christian point of view, which teaches that God hates break ups (Mal 2:16). In a union between a husband and wife Lord painfully permits divorce only on the grounds of unfaithfulness. What about organizational break ups, what are the terms, and can a follower earn an organizational divorce? Matthew 18:15–17 indicates that "if your brother sins against you, go and tell him his fault between you and him alone. If he hears you, you have gained your brother.[16] But if he will not

---

[1] Schaufeli, W. B., M Salanova, V. Gonzales-Roma, and A. B. Bakker. 2001. "The measurement of engagement and burnout: A two sample confirmatory factor analytic approach." *Journal of Happiness Studies* 3, 71–92.

hear, take with you one or two more, that *'by the mouth of two or three witnesses every word may be established.'*[17] And if he refuses to hear them, tell *it* to the church. But if he refuses even to hear the church, let him be to you like a heathen and a tax collector."

A close analysis of the Matthean 18:15–17 model reveals that several steps should be employed before one embraces the fourth boardroom language. An offended follower is instructed by Jesus to first go alone to the person and explain the fault between the two. What is interesting to note is that Christ does not put the onus for initiating a conversation on the person who did the offending but on the person who was offended. If this courageous act is not received by the other, the next step is to bring in two or three others to serve as witnesses to possibly help resolve the issue. However, if such gestures are unfruitful, a follower is charged with taking it to the church with the hope of arriving at a positive resolution. Finally, if such steps do not result in a positive outcome, one is then authorized to receive, if you would, an organizational divorce by treating them like a heathen and tax collector.

What does the phrase "treat them like a heathen and tax collector" mean? Gardner explains that this phrase means that believers should treat such a person "as one who stands outside the circle of faith. What is envisioned is not isolation from the sinner, but a radical redefinition of the relationship. From this point on, the community will no longer relate to the person as a fellow disciple, but as someone of the world who has yet to be discipled."[2] To this end, before a follower embarks upon the next boardroom language, it would be a wise move to explore if a follower has adhered to the Matthean 18:15–17 model and thereby earned an organizational divorce?

The final question that a follower should contemplate becomes, "Are you at peace or falling to pieces?" This play on words points to three scriptures. The first can be found in Romans 12:18–21,

If it is possible, as much as depends on you, live peaceably with all men.[19] Beloved, do not avenge yourselves, but *rather* give place to wrath; for it is written, *'Vengeance is Mine, I will repay,'* says the Lord.[20] Therefore *'If your enemy is hungry, feed him; If he is thirsty, give him a drink; For in so doing you will heap coals of fire on his head.'*[21] Do not be overcome by evil, but overcome evil with good.

---

[2] Gardner, R. B. (1991). *Matthew* (p. 281). Scottdale, PA: Herald Press.

94   M. A. BUFORD

The apex of this text is verse 18, *if it is possible, as much as depends on you, live peaceably with all*. An inference of this text is that there may be times where living peaceably is not possible, as illustrated by the previous conversation about an organizational divorce. What about a follower's internal peace?

To explore this question, the second text needs to be considered. Colossians 3:14–15 indicates that, "But above all these things put on love, which is the bond of perfection.[15] And let the peace of God rule in your hearts, to which also you were called in one body; and be thankful." As a follower robes themselves in *agapao* love and exercises an attitude of gratitude in all things, it should be noted that a pivotal principle of discernment is the peace of God ruling in one's heart. Stated differently, when a follower is inclined to take vengeance into their own hands, chances are they are actively falling to pieces and will be more of a hindrance than a help. In contrast, when a follower gives space to the principles of God, they will, in turn, be in a better place to discern the Lord's will, as indicated by peace ruling their heart. Plainly put, if one has a spiritual peace that passes all understanding about leaving, it is a high probability that the Lord is providing a clearance to proceed.

One can discover this reality being played out in the third passage that invokes the peace factor. Matthew 10:11–14 states, "Now whatever city or town you enter, inquire who in it is worthy, and stay there till you go out.[12] And when you go into a household, greet it.[13] If the household is worthy, let your peace come upon it. But if it is not worthy, let your peace return to you.[14] And whoever will not receive you nor hear your words, when you depart from that house or city, shake off the dust from your feet." Notice the relationship between peace, worthiness, and the decision point to leave. In this text, when an organization no longer fits a follower nor receives their words of counsel, Jesus indicated that his disciples should literally shake the dust from their feet. This symbolic act was a renunciation and indicated a severed relationship.[3] A synthesis of the passages within this section provides a theological construct that walking away wins the day.

---

[3] Barry, J. D., Mangum, D., Brown, D. R., Heiser, M. S., Custis, M., Ritzema, E., ... Bomar, D. (2012, 2016). *Faithlife Study Bible* (Mt 10:14). Bellingham, WA: Lexham Press.

The Theory and Psychology of Quitting

Although the literature is relatively silent with regard to the theory and psychology of quitting, two voices have distinguished themselves in the field. Ira Chaleff, in *The Courageous Follower: Standing Up To and For Our Leaders*, first outlines a sound theory of leaving. He contends that "Although moral action does not always require leaving a group or organization, it always implies the potential of leaving if the offending situation is not corrected or, indeed, if we ourselves have offended the core values of the group."[4] This assertion makes it clear that neither leader nor led are exempt from compromising core values or pondering the harsh realities of departing. Chaleff suggests there are several possible reasons that may cause a follower to want to leave, which include:

- **Growth**—A follower recognizes that they have reached a ceiling of learning and development. To further advance capacities, it may be advantageous for a follower to depart.
- **Group Optimization**—Chaleff argues that group optimization is coming to grasps with the fact that the team needs fresh eyes and blood to engage the system. By stepping aside on this premise, it recognizes that a follower can no longer add value to the group.
- **Exhaustion**—A follower essentially becomes burned out (debatably resulting from a poor person–job fit) and has lost a sense meaningfulness. Due to this new norm, Chaleff argues that the responsible act may be to leave.[5]
- **Principled Action**—If a follower has not been able to keep the trust, though it may not be logical, it would be the right thing to step aside.
- **Financial Contingencies**—Because most followers are not independently wealthy, Chaleff suggests the challenges of making a living may make one pause.

Before a follower decides to metaphorically "shake the dust off their shoes" and depart, that influencer should be advised of the emotional effects of this choice. Chaleff rightly asserts that "Separation difficulty is

---

[4] Chaleff, Ira. 1995. *The Courageous Follower: Standing Up To and For Our Leaders*. San Franciso: Berrett-Koehler Publishers, Inc. p. 150.
[5] Ibid. p. 152.

ultimately a crisis of identity."[6] This crisis of identity may be akin to couples making the difficult decision to go their separate ways after years of marriage. The grieving affiliated with carving out a new life without that person, the questions, and the fear of the unknown that lies around the corner may, unfortunately, keep some in the confines of an unhealthy wedlock, even though vows have been broken.

In this vein, the insights of Peg Streep and Alan Bernstein's book, *Quitting: Why We Fear It—and Why We Shouldn't—in Life, Love, and Work*, help to explain the psychology of why some will not depart an unhealthy work environment. These authors make a persuasive argument, particularly for citizens of the United States, that quitting goes against the very fiber of who we are. That is, it was the fight of the founders of the republic who refused to succumb to overwhelming odds. It is the messages we communicate, such as, winners never quit and quitters never win, that persuade the masses that quitting is never the answer. Moreover, the authors suggest that "the belief in persistence and the American Dream, a quitter is one of the strongest epithets you can toss at someone. It connotes a deep-seated character flaw, an inability to commit to a course, and weakness in the face of challenge."[7]

This line of thinking can potentially become a blind spot if a follower is not aware. To this end, the authors expand the understanding of this construct by suggesting that, "Artful quitting, by definition, involves letting go of the familiar, staking out new territory, living through a period of ambiguity, and dealing with the emotional fallout of letting go of something important."[8] In keeping with the essence of this book, this understanding of artful quitting is, by definition, a bold act that will require the assistance of God. This understanding of artful quitting sets the stage to take a hard look at the fourth boardroom language—*Step Down*.

REFLECTIVE LEADERSHIP

To recap a previous point, the boardroom language of stepping down applies to the leader as well as to the led. In light of this assertion, the ensuing discussion will intentionally explore both sides of the leader and follower spectrum when applicable, with an emphasis on whether remorse has emerged as for David in I Chronicles 21:17. "And David said to God, 'Was it not I who commanded the people to be numbered? I am the one who has sinned and done evil indeed; but these sheep, what have they

[6] Ibid. p. 153.
[7] Streep, Peg, and Alan Bernstein. 2014. *Quitting*. Philadelphia, PA: Da Capo Press. p. 8.
[8] Ibid. p. 10.

done? Let Your hand, I pray, O LORD my God, be against me and my father's house, but not against Your people that they should be plagued'." In this text, one can abstract a model for leadership remorse.

Reflective leadership occurs when an influencer first sincerely moves from king-think to inquiring of the Lord in prayer. This gesture shows brokenness, humility, and acknowledges the truth recorded in Proverbs 3:5–6, "Trust in the LORD with all your heart, And lean not on your own understanding;6 In all your ways acknowledge Him, And He shall direct your paths." The second aspect of reflective leadership is the ability to assume full responsibility for the predicament facing the organization. The leader or follower does not point fingers, nor seek to justify themself, on the contrary, they point out that the fault was theirs alone. Third, reflective leadership not only assumes responsibility, but also willingly accepts the full measure of the punishment. Finally, authentic, reflective leadership tries to make it right in the end by putting the best interests of the led before self.

RESIST UNTIL FIRED

In keeping with the spirit of previous boardroom languages, the first form of stepping down is to *resist until fired* as depicted in Fig. 6.1. This course of action assumes that the led accept that removal from their position is

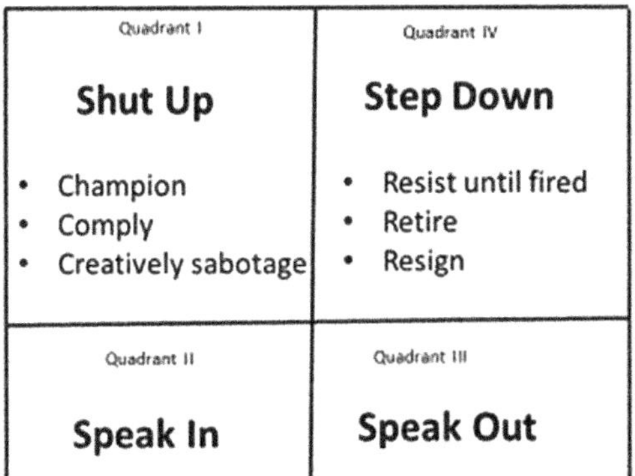

Quadrant I	Quadrant IV
Shut Up	**Step Down**
• Champion • Comply • Creatively sabotage	• Resist until fired • Retire • Resign
Quadrant II	Quadrant III
Speak In	**Speak Out**
• Parable • Pack • Principles	• Whine • Whisper • Whistle blow

Fig. 6.1 Boardroom boldness language model—quadrant IV

imminent. From the perspective of the follower, instead of passively accepting this reality and assuming the pending firing is unjust, followers can band together to resist with a strike. Employing the method of a collective work stoppage in response to a wrong can send a powerful message as productivity comes to streaking halt. This was the thinking that fueled some employees at Walmart. On October 12, 2012, some 88 workers from 28 Walmart sites in various cities organized a strike. Although their technique was unconventional (the followers had a strike for one day but returned to work the next), they were organized, and rallied around a single purpose. Their focus was twofold. First, to build momentum over the coming weeks for a planned massive walkout on Black Friday—the biggest shopping day of the year.[9] Second, to end retaliation against Walmart employees who complain about working conditions or attempt to organize.[10]

What was the outcome of the strike to stop management retaliation against employees who speak up? What lessons can one glean from the Walmart case? Some of the followers' demands were met by leadership and conditions did improve. In the sentiments of one reporter, "Ready to walk out of your job? Hold on. Before you run out the door, here's what you need to know about your right to protest your working condition."[11] According to Donna Ballman:

- **Supervisors can't protest**: ... the National Labor Relations Act doesn't apply…
- **There is safety in numbers**:… with at least one co-worker, then you may be legally protected.
- **You are guaranteed an equivalent job if management fills the position while you're striking**: If [the strike is] to seek higher wages, shorter hours, or better working conditions, then you are an "economic striker." That means you are legally protected from being fired, but not being permanently replaced…
- **You can complain to co-workers about your grievances**…
- **Filing a formal complaint to the government will protect you**[12]

[9] Gordon, Claire. 2012. "Walmart Workers: This Is Why We're Striking And Making Black Friday Threat." *AOL Finance.* October 11. Accessed November 12, 2017. https://www.aol.com/2012/10/11/walmart-workers-this-is-why-were-striking-and-making-black-fri/
[10] Ibid.
[11] Ballman, Donna. 2012. "Why Walmart Won't Fire Striking Workers—And What That Means For You." *AOL FINANCE.* October 15. Accessed November 12, 2017. https://www.aol.com/2012/10/15/walmart-striking-workers-non-unionized/

WALKING AWAY TO WIN THE DAY **99**

The other side of the *resist until fired* coin is at an individual level. Instead of striking to draw public attention to a grievance, one can also leverage the firing moment to help dramatize injustice with the hope of swaying public opinion for the purposes of change. A historical example of this form of boardroom language is known as the Saturday Night Massacre. During President Richard Nixon's administration, there was a break-in at the Democratic National Committee's office at a hotel known as Watergate. In response to this 1972 incident, a formal investigation was initiated by U.S. Attorney General Elliot Richardson. Richardson, in turn, stood up as an independent special prosecutor and named Archibald Cox as the primary, who issued a subpoena to the President. President Nixon refused the summons and later approached the Attorney General and ordered the investigation to be halted. When both Archibald Cox and Elliot Richardson resisted, they were both fired for "defiance."[13]

What is interesting to note was how the collective minds of the American population shifted as a result of Watergate and the firings. According to Bumb, this issue eroded the confidence of voters and, debatably, became the catalyst for President Nixon's resignation.[14] However, speaking the language of resisting until fired comes at a price. In the sentiments of Martin Luther King, Jr., "I have lived these last few years with the conviction that *unearned suffering is redemptive.*" Analogously, resisting until fired can indeed be a redemptive nonviolent act for others but comes with pain as a follower stands on truth.

A leader who has embraced king-thinking does not have the option to convey this boardroom language with the hope of a positive outcome. This assertion is largely because such resisting is predicated on a lie or immoral practice. The firing moment will indeed come, but it is more than likely to end in a comparable way to David's predecessor, Saul, when he fell on his sword (1 Sam 31:4). The blind spot affiliated with Saul's pride may have convinced him in a narcissistic way to not go down without a fight. It is this line of thinking, laced with living in yesterday's glory, that keeps such leaders from seeing that they are the reason for the negative organizational trends.

[12] Ibid.
[13] Kneeland, Douglas E. 1973. "Nixon Discharges Cox For Defiance; Abolishes Watergate Task Force, Richardson And Ruckelshaus Out." *New York Times,* October 23. Accessed November 12, 2017. http://www.nytimes.com/learning/general/onthisday/big/1020.html#article
[14] Bump, Philip. 2017. "How America viewed the Watergate scandal, as it was unfolding." *The Washington Post.* 15 May. Accessed November 12, 2017. https://www.washingtonpost.

RETIRE

The second form of the step down boardroom language is to *retire*. The dictionary defines retirement as the action or fact of leaving one's job and ceasing to work. This is an option for some, but not necessarily for all. The demands of making a living, supporting a family, not having enough seniority, nor a solid nest egg may keep this door closed for most. However, if a follower has been diligent in their planning, they have the seniority, and the mandate; submitting one's papers for retirement could potentially serve two purposes. As alluded to before, first, this pathway can send a strong message to the team, particularly if one has distinguished oneself. This gesture of announcing retirement due to the toxicity of leadership may be the spur that others need to rise above the apathy. On the other side of the coin, the tool of retirement may provide the organization with new blood, fresh eyes, and the renewed energy to ask tough questions about the status quo. Given the fact that more people are working beyond the age of 70, this seems to suggest that retirement may not be for all.[15]

RESIGN

The final element of the step down boardroom language is to *resign*. William F. Felice, in *How do I Save My Honor? War, Moral Integrity, and Principled Resignation*, makes a compelling case for principled resignation. He contends that "an ethic of principled resignation would serve to support habits of personal integrity and moral autonomy. Such an ethic is based on the idea that the primary duty of all government employees and all citizens is to individual conscience."[16] Felice goes on to argue that most organizations, regrettably, place more capital on loyalty to the team as opposed to the right. Although most times they align, the time that they do not can be problematic. Thus, as the following cases will illustrate, the boardroom language of resigning can be a powerful, principled tool in the hand of the leader, as well as the led, if employed correctly.

com/news/politics/wp/2017/05/15/how-america-viewed-the-watergate-scandal-as-it-was-unfolding/?utm_term=.8c39e9820c6c

[15] Boschma, Janie. 2015. "When Do Americans Think They'll Actually Retire?" *The Atlantic*. June 23. Accessed November 13, 2017. https://www.theatlantic.com/business/archive/2015/06/ideal-retirement-age-work/396464/

[16] Felice, William F. 2009. *How Do I Save My Honor? War, Moral Integrity, and Principled Resignation*. Lanham: Rowman & Littlefield Publishers, Inc. [Kindle Loc 2894].

The Case of William Ruchelshaus

To return to the story of President Nixon's apparent attempt to cover up improprieties; the President ordered the Attorney General to fire special prosecutor Cox in the Watergate investigation. When Elliot Richardson refused, the President relieved him of duty. The next person in the chain of command was the Deputy Attorney General, William Ruckelshaus. When approached by the President in the same fashion, Ruckelshaus decided to exercise the boardroom language of stepping down and submitted his formal letter of resignation. This simple gesture demonstrated profound courage and loyalty, not to a person but to a higher moral standard. As history reflects and analyzes the events of that day, one would have to say that the bold followership of Richardson, Ruckelshaus, and Cox was the needed prescription for a sick culture.

The Case of Fred Price Jr.'s Resignation

The boardroom language of *resigning* also applies to the leadership. This language can become a healthy pathway for organization and leader if handled with grace, boldness, and with the intent to become healthy again. Consider the case of Fred Price Jr. The son of pastor Fred C. Price of the Crenshaw Christian Center was appointed by his father as the pastor of the 28,000-member congregation in 2009. After serving for eight years Fred Price Jr., took approximately a month's sabbatical from the ministry.[17] Upon his return, with his bride by his side, Price Jr. made the following statement to the members of Crenshaw Christian Center.

> Approximately a month ago I came before you to announce that I would be taking a three-week sabbatical. Well I'm here today to give you an update. I have struggled with and am correcting and making amends for serious personal misjudgments which have affected my life and my family and which I deeply regret. I have betrayed the trust of God, my family and you my church and for that I am so sorry. Therefore, I'm gonna step down as pastor at this time, in order to fulfill the call on my life to ministry. I have submitted myself to my fathers, our apostles' plan of restoration, chief among those is

[17]Blair, Leonardo. 2017. "Calif. Megachurch Pastor Fred Price Jr. Steps Down Over 'Personal Misjudgments'." *Christianpost.com*. June 27. Accessed November 13, 2017. https://www.christianpost.com/news/crenshaw-christian-center-pastor-fred-price-jr-steps-down-over-personal-misjudgments-189765/

102   M. A. BUFORD

I will be attending Sunday service starting next week and throughout the year, so that I can hear the Word and be restored in order to fulfill the call on my life to ministry. In closing I would like to ask that you respect my family's privacy while we work through this personal situation. I thank you all for the support you have given me. As pastor, I love you all and I solicit your prayers during this difficult time.[18]

An examination of Fred Price Jr.'s resignation reveals several things. First, one can infer that during his sabbatical, he engaged in some intense soul searching, counseling, and time in prayer. Seemingly this season of leave was not enough to resolve his issues. The second item that can be lifted from his resignation is an acknowledgment of his "serious personal misjudgments." Such misjudgments had impacted God, his family, the church, and his self. Third, that there was a plan of restoration in place and that such a strategy involved the ministry of the Word of God. Finally, Price Jr. solicited the prayers of the saints during his time of healing. Perhaps this is the twenty-first-century template (see Chap. 1 for a more in-depth perspective) for leaders to be restored? Although such renewal may not necessarily equal being placed back into the same position, it should mean being restored back into the right fellowship with God. As the leader or the led first seek the kingdom of God and all His righteousness, these things will be added (Matt 6:33).

The Case of Washington's Resignation

On the other side of the coin, resignations do not have to be spurred on by misjudgments. On the contrary, leaders can exercise sound judgment to discern the times and understand that such a move is the right thing to do because it is the right thing to do. A shining, historical beacon of this is President George Washington. Upon being voted in as the first leader of the United States of America and after enjoying a triumphant victory over Britain, Washington made the call to step down and away from the levers of power. Before mandatory term limits were written into the Amendment of the Constitution, this leader had the vision to see what was best for democracy. In a speech given on December 23, 1783, he proclaimed the following:

[18] Ibid.

WALKING AWAY TO WIN THE DAY   103

The great events on which my resignation depended having at length taken place; I have now the honor of offering my sincere Congratulations to Congress and of presenting myself before them to surrender into their hands the trust committed to me, and to claim the indulgence of retiring from the Service of my Country. Happy in the confirmation of our Independence and Sovereignty, and pleased with the opportunity afforded the United States of becoming a respectable Nation, I resign with satisfaction the Appointment I accepted with diffidence. A diffidence in my abilities to accomplish so arduous a task, which however was superseded by a confidence in the rectitude of our Cause, the support of the Supreme Power of the Union, and the patronage of Heaven.

The Successful termination of the War has verified the most sanguine expectations, and my gratitude for the interposition of Providence, and the assistance I have received from my Countrymen, increases with every review of the momentous Contest. While I repeat my obligations to the Army in general, I should do injustice to my own feelings not to acknowledge in this place the peculiar Services and distinguished merits of the Gentlemen who have been attached to my person during the War. It was impossible the choice of confidential Officers to compose my family should have been more fortunate. Permit me Sir, to recommend in particular those, who have continued in Service to the present moment, as worthy of the favorable notice and patronage of Congress.

I consider it an indispensable duty to close this last solemn act of my Official life, by commending the Interests of our dearest Country to the protection of Almighty God, and those who have the superintendence of them, to his holy keeping. Having now finished the work assigned me, I retire from the great theatre of Action; and bidding an Affectionate farewell to this August body under whose orders I have so long acted, I here offer my Commission, and take my leave of all the employments of public life.[19]

What enabled Washington to depart with grace and speak this boardroom language with a moral clarity? Washington understood that his position of leadership was a trust bestowed upon him by divine providence and the will of the people. When a leader views themself as a steward and not an owner of an organization, resigning for the health of the team becomes as natural as breathing. However, when a leader envi-

[19]Washington, George. 1783. "George Washinton Speech." *Maryland Archives.* December 23. Accessed November 13, 2017. https://www.google.com/search?source=hp&ei=h18JWsL-LMHSmwGZy4ugAg&q=george+washington+resignation+speech&oq=George+Washingto n+res&gs_l=psy-ab.1.3.0l10.2723.12701.0.16959.25.23.2.0.0.0.106.1923. 19j3.22.0....0...1.1.64.psy-ab..1.24.1973...46j0i131k1j0i10k1j

sions themself as the owner and entailed to power, problems begin to emerge that cause mayhem in the life of others. This tendency, unfortunately, blinds a leader from discerning the truth of Ecclesiastes 3:1–2, "To everything, there is a season, a time for every purpose under the heaven... A time to plant, and a time to pluck what is planted." The question now becomes, in what season of your organizational life do you find yourself?

BOARDROOM BOLDNESS CHATS

The Case of Are You With Them or With Me?

You are a senior ranking staffer in the President's Cabinet. The nation is still grieving the loss of life after the evil attacks on America on 9/11. As the dust begins to settle and intelligence reports surface, you are presented with inconclusive data. The conventional wisdom in the cabinet is to act on the intel of Iraq having weapons of mass destruction and that they may be the culprits who attacked. The top leadership seems to be leaning aggressively toward going to war but would like the cabinet to be of one accord. Moreover, you have noticed how others were unfairly being painted as unpatriotic if they dissented. You cannot, in good conscience, give your consent due to the lack of evidence and the skewed tunnel vision of the leader. The leader wants to know, "Are you with them or with me?"

1. While reflecting on the case of *are you with them or with me*, have a discussion on the theology, psychology, and philosophy of quitting.
2. Have a discussion on the meaning and the possible application of leadership remorse in this case. Within your discussion, be sure to think through the implications of a leader who refuses to be remorseful.
3. Have a discussion on the meaning and the possible application of *resisting until being fired* fired as depicted in Fig. 6.2. in this case. Within your discussion, role play how this may or may not help.

Fig. 6.2   The spectrum of the "step-down" boardroom language

4. Have a discussion on the meaning and the possible application of how *retiring* may or may not help the organization. Within your dialog be sure to discuss in detail the impact this may have on the family too.
5. Have a conversation on the leader as well as the led usage of *resignation*.

CHAPTER 7

If It Is to Be, It Is Left Up to We: The People, by People, and for the People

THE FIFTH BOARDROOM LANGUAGE

The final boardroom boldness language is to *step it up* as depicted in figure 7.1. This principle can be found in the latter part of 1 Chronicles 21:16, "Then David lifted his eyes and saw the angel of the LORD standing between earth and heaven, having in his hand a drawn sword stretched out over Jerusalem. So David and the elders, clothed in sackcloth, fell on their faces." For the first time in the text, one can discover the activity and initiative of the elders. Seemingly these senior statesmen of the nation had seen enough destruction, were done with being passive followers and were now ready to step it up with engaged followership. However, the question becomes, "What specifically does step it up look like for the twenty-first-century influencer?" To answer this question, the attention of the reader will be focused on the biblical case of Moses as the nation of Israel was battling Amalek.

> And so it was, when Moses held up his hand, that Israel prevailed; and when he let down his hand, Amalek prevailed.[12] But Moses' hands *became* heavy; so they took a stone and put *it* under him, and he sat on it. And Aaron and Hur supported his hands, one on one side, and the other on the other side; and his hands were steady until the going down of the sun.[13] So Joshua defeated Amalek and his people with the edge of the sword. (Ex 17:11–13)

© The Author(s) 2018   107
M. A. Buford, *Bold Followership*, Christian Faith Perspectives in Leadership and Business, https://doi.org/10.1007/978-3-319-74530-5_7

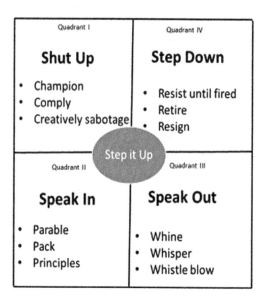

Fig. 7.1 Boardroom boldness language model—quadrant V

Unity of Effort

The first lesson that can be abstracted from the elders in this text is that these followers understood that they were the difference between national failure and victory. As Aaron and Hur watched the momentum of the fight change to the opposition, it was as if they knew they were the key. No one else had the status, the proximity to the leader, or the wisdom to navigate the moment. In a similar vein, this was the predicament of the elders around David as they saw the angel of the LORD standing between earth and heaven, having in his hand a drawn sword stretched out over Jerusalem. When history calls, bold followers understand that they become Plan A, and that Plan B was to make Plan A work.

The success or demise of a Plan A hinges on how well bold followers step it up with a unity of effort. Paul Michael Severance's doctoral dissertation, *Characterizing the Construct of Organizational Unity of Effort in the Interagency National Security Policy Process*, provides a framework for this construct. Severance explains that "unity of effort in this respect essentially establishes who does what to whom."[1] Moreover, Severance's research unearths a model that can help followers formulate the appropriate engagement approach. The first component of the model is strategic orientation, in which it is imperative for the team to have a clearly defined and integrated strategy, and that team members are fully invested up and down the chain of command. Additionally, the strategic orientation needs to be grounded on a compelling vision for the future that is book-ended with clear goals, objectives, purposes, and mission.

The second element of Severance's model is organizational context and interpersonal dynamics. The premise of this leg of the unity of effort can arguably be tied to 1 Thessalonians 5:12–13, in which the Apostle Paul admonishes, "to know them which labor among you, and are over you in the Lord, and admonish you; And to esteem them very highly in love for their work's sake. *And* be at peace among yourselves." The operative word in this text is *know them*, οἶδα, which can be translated as to examine, inspect, or to make an acquaintance. The result of adhering to this theological mandate is the elevation of trust, rapport, respect, and a richer understanding of the values of the team. Additionally, Severance encourages meaningful interagency training and education.

The third and perhaps most critical aspect of the model is the leadership and decision-making structure. Key questions have to be resolved, "What will the lines of authority be? What would be the directive of such authority and what would be the nature and the flow of leadership?" In a similar vein, the final leg of this model would be the organizational infrastructure and resources. That is, followers need to understand the budgets associated with the engagement, exactly who and how it would be funded. The entity would need to think through measures of effectiveness and how the organization will say thank you, as well as how to motivate her citizens.

As indicated at the beginning of this chapter, Genesis 11:6 reveals the power of unity of effort. To recap, "And the LORD said, 'Indeed the people *are* one, and they all have one language, and this is what they begin to do; now nothing that they propose to do will be withheld from them'." In this text, the entire world was one and spoke the same language. Unfortunately, their strategic orientation was flawed, as epitomized by their desire to build a city, to build a tower up to heaven, and to make a

---

[1] Severance, Paul Michael. 2005. *Characterizing the Construct of Organizational Unity of Effort in the Interagency National Security Policy Process*. Falls Virginia: Proquest Doctoral Dissertation. p. 6.

name for themselves (Gen 11:4). Although this was not the will of God for them, the Lord acknowledged that when people are one—nothing that they propose to do will be withheld from them.

THE FIERCE URGENCY OF NOW

What the reader will not discover in the Exodus 17:11–13 passage is a competition for recognition. On the contrary, these elders seemingly could not care less who got the credit as long as God received the glory. Such a mindset is often the byproduct of the fierce urgency of now. Martin Luther King Jr. best captured the meaning of this second concept when he said, "We are now faced with the fact that tomorrow is today. We are confronted with the fierce urgency of now. In this unfolding conundrum of life and history, there 'is' such a thing as being too late. This is not time for apathy or complacency. This is a time for vigorous and positive action." When followers embrace the mindset that tomorrow is today, a bias for action naturally springs forth.

John P. Kotter, in *A Sense of Urgency*, explains the urgency principle with more granularity. More specifically, Kotter's research discovered that one could invoke four tactics to help create earnestness. The first concept revolves around bringing the *outside in*. This phrase points toward moving an organization from being complacent by only looking within at past accomplishments, as opposed to exploring outward possibilities. Second, Kotter contends that one should behave with urgency every day. This posture could be a contagious gesture to help keep the passion burning within to accomplish the mission. The third finding of Kotter's revolved around the notion of finding opportunities in crises. Whenever change is being incorporated, there is a high probability of strategy not surviving initial contact. To this end, the urgent follower understands how to locate chance in the midst of chaos. Finally, Kotter contends that one can keep applying urgency by incorporating resolve into the culture.

More practically speaking, the fierce urgency of now can be likened to a house being on fire with people inside. Because of the threat of flames and smoke, the people within the home have a single perspective, to leave that house safely and then to put the flames out quickly. The urgency of the moment that was created by the blaze suspends any hidden agendas, tames out of control egos, and galvanizes everyone to keep to the main thing. In this spirit, Aaron and Hur, and the elders around David, understood that their "house" was burning and moved with a sense of urgency to get out of the threat and to suppress the flames.

Fasting and Prayer

Aaron and Hur intuitively understood that victory had little to do with the warfare tactics of the forces under Joshua's leadership and more to do with being connected to the Lord. To this end, these bold followers activated the third aspect of the *step it up* boardroom language—fasting and prayer. These followers quickly made the connection of Moses' arms being lifted as a picture of prayer. Due to Aaron's role as the first high priest of Israel, one could reasonably infer that this follower was well acquainted with the power of fasting and prayer. As recorded in Mark 9:14–29, a man brought his son to Jesus' disciples that had a condition that caused him to throw himself down, foam at the mouth, gnash his teeth, and make him rigid. The disciples were unable to help the child, so the parent brought his son to Jesus, who exercised his authority and healed the child. Later, Jesus explained to his disciples why they were unsuccessful by saying, "This kind can come out by nothing but prayer and fasting."

This component of the step it up boardroom language can be utilized strategically. To illustrate, the book of Esther explains that a sinister plot was set in motion to commit genocide on the entire nation of Israel. Esther, was divinely positioned as the new queen but her Jewish nationality was concealed. At the appropriate moment her mentor and cousin, Mordecai, advised her in Esther 4:13–14 of the plot by saying, "Do not think in your heart that you will escape in the king's palace any more than all the other Jews. For if you remain completely silent at this time, relief and deliverance will arise for the Jews from another place, but you and your father's house will perish. Yet who knows whether you have come to the kingdom for *such* a time as this?" Esther's response of was not that of panic nor of human endeavor. On the contrary, Esther replied to Mordecai by saying, in verse 16, "Go, gather all the Jews who are present in Shushan, and fast for me; neither eat nor drink for three days, night or day. My maids and I will fast likewise. And so I will go to the king, which *is* against the law; and if I perish, I perish!" It was this follower's boldness, coupled with the language of fasting and prayer, that allowed God to intervene.

One can also see this form of stepping it up emerge early in the Constitutional Convention of 1787. As the newly liberated country struggled to draft the right language that would guide the country forward, the efforts of the founding fathers were frustrated. It was within the context of being foiled that Benjamin Franklin admonished the framers to pray. He specifically exhorted the assembly with the following words,

112 M. A. BUFORD

In this situation of this Assembly, groping as it were in the dark to find political truth, and scarce able to distinguish it when presented to us, how has it happened, sir, that we have not hitherto once thought of humbly applying to the Father of Lights to illuminate our understanding? In the beginning of the contest with Great Britain, when we were sensible of danger, we had daily prayer in this room for the Divine protection. Our prayers, sir, were heard, and they were graciously answered. All of us who were engaged in the struggle must have observed frequent instances of a superintending Providence in our favor... And have we now forgotten that powerful Friend? Or do we imagine we no longer need His assistance? I have lived, sir, a long time, and the longer I live, the more convincing proofs I see of this truth – that God governs in the affairs of men. And if a sparrow cannot fall to the ground without His notice, is it probable that an empire can rise without His aid? We have been assured, sir, in the Sacred Writings, that 'except the Lord build the House, they labor in vain that build it.' I firmly believe this; and I also believe that without His concurring aid we shall succeed in this political building no better than the builders of Babel. I therefore beg leave to move that henceforth prayers imploring the assistance of Heaven, and its blessings on our deliberations, be held in this Assembly every morning before we proceed to business.[2]

The outcome of this admonishment has set democracy on the path that has surpassed the imaginations of the naysayers.

PROACTIVITY

Akin to fasting and praying is the fourth aspect of stepping it up—proactivity. Stephen R. Covey, in his classic book *The 7 Habits Of Highly Effective People: Powerful Lessons In Personal Change* defines proactivity in a distinguished manner. Covey suggests that it is the ability to subordinate an impulse to a value or to understand that a person is "response-able" or has the responsibility to use their resources and initiative to answer a problem.[3] Moreover, proactive people are not driven by feelings, by circumstance, by conditions, or by their environment.[4] Although the atmosphere that Aaron and Hur saw was indeed bleak, they did not choose to play the

---

[2] Farrand, Max. 1911. *The Records of the Federal Convention of 1787, Vol. I.* New Haven: Yale University Press. pp. 450–452, from James Madison's notes on the Convention for June 28, 1787.

[3] Covey, Stephen R. 2013. *The 7 Habits Of Highly Effective People: Powerful Lessons In Personal Change.* New York: RosettaBooks.

[4] Ibid. p. 79.

blame game and spend precious amounts of time assigning fault. Neither did these followers default to that favorite conventional pastime of criticizing and pointing out obvious problems. On the contrary, Aaron and Hur stepped it up by using their resourcefulness and initiative to make an impact. How? They located a stone and put it under Moses, and they used their strength to support the hands of their leader until the battle was won.

Project Bold Followership

As the reader's attention is returned to the elders around David, there seems to be a model that followers can embrace to positively influence today's organizations that are being crippled by king-think. If a leader refuses to become reflective, even though the team is on the brink of demise, then the organization's citizens are morally bound to step it up and shape the conditions for a nonviolent workplace revolution. The etymology of the word revolution means to revolve, rotate or to roll back. As depicted in Figure 7.2, the step it up model synthesizes the various constructs unearthed in this study to mitigate mayhem.

Said another way, there are leaders within organizations who are running followers, team legacy, and fundamental values to the ground, all in the name of egoism. Organizational citizens do not have to witness and softly endorse such madness by remaining silent and passive. On the contrary, followers do have the power to rotate, revolve, and even roll back the likes of the modern-day Jim Jones, Jeffery Skilling, and Ken Lay out of power. The findings of this book suggest that when followers coalesce around a clear unity of effort, in the sentiments of the Lord, "nothing that they propose to do will be withheld from them." (Gen 11:6) This mindset, coupled with a fierce urgency of now, can help influencers to realize

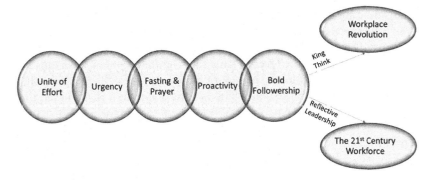

Fig. 7.2 The step it up model

that there "is" such a thing as being too late. When a follower accepts this reality, they can appeal higher with fasting and prayer for who knows what; they too may have come into the kingdom for such a time as this.

After followers, like the founding fathers at the Constitutional Conference, fervently seek the mind of God, they must rise from their knees and proactively engage with bold followership. More specifically, organizational citizens can speak with one voice and stage project bold followership (PBF). PBF can be defined as speaking nonviolently and simultaneously a hybrid of the boardroom boldness language in the organization until revolution ensues. That is, a proportion of followers can begin to speak the specific boardroom language of *shut up* as they *creatively sabotage* immoral practices implemented by leaders. Concurrently, those providentially placed within the king's court can first study to understand the king's preferred communication method and then boldly *speak in,* which should invoke a *parable,* embrace *packs* or *principles,* the message must be clear.

While a portion of the team is shutting up with the principles of creative sabotaging and speaking in, other key followers can massively *speak out.* The acts of *whispering* and *whistleblowing* can help to bring dark issues to the light for the purposes of pricking public conscience. Moreover, influential followers in the leader's administration can elect to *step down* due to the ethical climate that has been established. The sum total is to help to create the conditions for transformation with nonviolent means before employing direct action if a sustained campaign has carefully: (1) collected facts to determine whether injustices are alive; (2) negotiated to resolve the leader and led issues; (3) employed self-purification to assure it is not a followership issue.

LEADING A TWENTY-FIRST-CENTURY ORGANIZATION

One of the interesting things to note at this point is the amount of energy, time, and capital that would be required to get a leader to become reflective. Nevertheless, such an effort would be well worth the proceeding if the lives of the team are positively enhanced. Assuming PBF achieves the objective of breaking the fever of king-think and moves such a personality to a place of remorsefulness, the question now becomes, "Is the only solution to accept their resignation?" This is a tricky question that will require the collective discernment of the followers of the campaign. What it is clearer to resolve entails the caliber of leadership for the twenty-first-century organization.

As the globe becomes flatter, the speed of information increases, and trust becomes the new currency, the role and voice of followership will be paramount. To effectively mobilize the talent and release the power of *we the people*, the personality entrusted with leading teams in the future must be reflective. Reflective leaders see themselves as stewards of treasures, not as saviors who are entitled to special treatment. A stewardship perspective acknowledges that one has been given temporary authority to care for a thing and has an obligation to return what was entrusted, in a better condition. Additionally, reflective leaders have a natural propensity to serve followers first, the organization next, and have a bias for organizational and personal learning. It is upon the pathway of pressing toward the mark (Phil 3:14), or being committed to personal learning, that one becomes self-aware of ones little foxes, grows, reconciles when wrong, and challenges others to walk in excellence as one strives for the same bar of righteousness.

As illustrated in Figure 7.3, reflective leadership champions organizational learning by keeping an ear first on the voice of God and then on the boardroom languages of followership. More specifically, when followers begin to *shut up*, reflective influencers *lead with prudent questions* to try to connect with the hearts of the people. When team members in the inner court begin to speak in boldly, the reflective influencer *listens with empathy*. This gesture, when done sincerely, conveys a powerful message of value to the communicator. When followers begin to speak out actively, those entrusted with being a steward of an institution will *learn with a level head*. This ability to not get defensive nor appalled about the voices

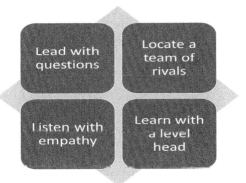

Fig. 7.3 The reflective leadership model

of the marginalized, but rather to learn about the "why" is a key trademark of a reflective leader.

When the elders of an institution begin to *step down* by submitting conscientious letters of resignation, reflective leaders *locate a team of rivals*. Because they are secure, wise, and humble enough to know that there is wisdom in a multitude of counselors (Pro 16:22), these leaders actively seek out those who think critically (i.e., challenge principles) but do not have a critical spirit (i.e., demean people's character out of spite). Finally, when followers begin to step it up aggressively, reflective leaders *leverage with empowerment*. Said differently, those vested with the special trust and confidence to lead the twenty-first-century organization understand that the ultimate success of the team will not flow from the top down but from the grassroots of we the people, by the people, and for the people.

BOARDROOM BOLDNESS CHATS

#MeToo

It has come to your attention that someone in top leadership sexually assaulted a person in your organization whom you have mentored for the past four years. The accused has been in power for one year and by all accounts seems to be doing a good job administratively. You have actionable knowledge that at least nine other people were victimized by this leader but are afraid to engage because they do not want to lose their jobs and do not necessarily want the attention; but you also know that others will be traumatized if nothing happens. Your mentee mentions a campaign called #MeToo and reluctantly signals they would like to do something, but need your help.

Fig. 7.4   The spectrum of the "step it up" boardroom language

1. While reflecting on the case of #MeToo, have a discussion on what the victim's options and the implications of doing nothing are.
2. Have a discussion on the meaning and the possible application of *stepping it up* in this case. Within your discussion, be sure to think through the implications of a leader who refuses to be remorseful.
3. Have a discussion on the implications of such a person becoming a reflective leader. Is reflection enough to keep that person in power, or should they be forced to resign?
4. Have a discussion on the most crucial element of the *step it up model* as depicted in Fig. 7.4 and why?
5. As organizations engage with the future, have a discussion on the importance of reflective leadership being at the helm.

CHAPTER 8

Measuring Your Organization's Boardroom Language

Thus far, this book has explored the boardroom language of David's advisers, more specifically, the actions of Joab, commander of the royal army, were closely scrutinized to understand better the dilemma of serving kingthink. Next, the personality of Gad was explored for how to speak in the life of a person blinded by narcissism. While discussing the ramifications of organizational dis-eases, this book utilized the literature to understand best practices for speaking out against immoral behaviours, particularly in a nonviolent way. Additionally, this study confronted the reality that often the best prescription to break the fever of organizational dis-ease is to shake up the top executives or convince them of the nobility of stepping down. Finally, the role of organizational elders was discussed, and it was pointed out that at the end of the day, the people had the influence to turn the ship around. The question became, "Were they willing to step it up?"

As entities prepare to navigate the plethora of challenges affiliated with a twenty-first-century workforce, it would be an unwise gesture to expect top executives to have all the answers and to be constantly on top of their game. For organizations to thrive in the information age, those who sit around the literal or metaphorical boardroom must find and activate their voice. This voice could very well be the difference between success and defeat, relevance or irrelevance, life and death. If the premise of this book is that boardroom boldness is the ultimate competitive edge, the question before the reader now becomes, "What is the organization's boardroom language of your team?" It has been determined that there are five concepts affiliated

© The Author(s) 2018
119
M. A. Buford, *Bold Followership*, Christian Faith Perspectives in Leadership and Business, https://doi.org/10.1007/978-3-319-74530-5_8

120 M. A. BUFORD

with Boardroom Boldness. The following is an attempt to understand if there are one or more scales that support the theory of this book.

THE BOARDROOM BOLDNESS LANGUAGE SCALE

In the context of the information age and the onslaught of tools such as Total Quality Management, Process Management, and Six Sigma Lean, it can be argued that unless one is adequately taking a measure of work, it is not leadership. To the credit of practitioners and scholars, the literature has shifted from merely watching the bottom line to monitoring the overall organization. To illustrate, Frost suggests that organizations are now inquiring about four key elements, which the Balanced Scorecard Model wants to understand:

- Financial—How do we look to shareholders?
- Processes—Are we improving how work is done?
- Growth—Are we renewing for continued growth?
- Customers—How do we look to our customers?[1]

The challenge of this book is to embrace a Balanced Scorecard approach that sufficiently addresses the research question and produces a reliable and a validated scale to measure corporate boardroom boldness languages. Such an endeavor could help to mitigate ethical mishaps and help organizations to optimize performance proactively (Tables 8.1, 8.2, 8.3).

STEP 1: DETERMINE CLEARLY WHAT IT IS YOU WANT TO MEASURE

The development of boardroom boldness scale(s) utilized the guidance of DeVellis, who contends that the construction of a tool to measure a phenomenon should adhere to eight guidelines. The first step involves determining clearly what it is one wants to measure. Although this is an obvious point, DeVellis encourages the researcher to think through questions such as, "Should the scale be based on theory, or should you strike out in new intellectual directions? How specific should the measure be? Should some aspect of the phenomenon be emphasized more than others?"[2]

[1] Frost, Bob. 2000. *Measuring Performance*. Dallas, TX: Measurement International.
[2] Devellis, Robert F. 2003. *Scale Development Theory and Applications*. London: Sage Publications.

MEASURING YOUR ORGANIZATION'S BOARDROOM LANGUAGE   121

Table 8.1   Boardroom boldness items

Item no	Item	Concept	Source
1	If my leader gives me an unethical order, I will salute and give it a 101 percent effort to accomplish the mission	Shut up	Lindsay (2012)
2	Unethical orders should be accomplished with extraordinary effort	Shut up	Lindsay (2012)
3	It is my duty to not only comply with an unethical order but to go one step beyond it	Shut up	Lindsay (2012)
4	If given the opportunity to champion an unethical order from a leader I respect, I will gladly execute it and go one step further	Shut up	Lindsay (2012)
5	If my leader issues me an immoral order, I will salute and give it a bare minimum effort to accomplish the mission	Shut up	Gibney (2005)
6	Immoral orders should be accomplished with bare minimum effort	Shut up	Gibney (2005)
7	It is my duty to comply with an immoral order	Shut up	Gibney (2005)
8	If given the opportunity to comply with an immoral order from a leader I respect, I will execute it and do nothing more	Shut up	Gibney (2005)
9	If my leader directs me to accomplish an unprincipled mission, I will secretly try to sabotage it innovately	Shut up	I Chr 21:4–6
10	Unprincipled orders should be sabotaged with creative energy	Shut up	I Chr 21:4–6
11	It is my duty to not only disrupt an unprincipled order but to also undermine it in a unique manner	Shut up	I Chr 21:4–6
12	If given the opportunity to interrupt an unprincipled order from a leader I respect, I would use my best imaginative option to stop it	Shut up	I Chr 21:4–6
13	When communicating with my direct supervisor, I prefer to use stories to try to change their point of view, particularly when they are wrong	Speak in	Copenhaver (1994)
14	When my organization is confronted with an ethical dilemma, the best course of action to help my leader to change is with an appropriate story	Speak in	Copenhaver (1994)
15	When a relevant historical narrative is provided to my leader, it can help them to make a moral decision	Speak in	Copenhaver (1994)
16	If my leader directs me to accomplish an unprincipled mission, I would use a values-based story to convince them to rescind the order	Speak in	Copenhaver (1994)

(*continued*)

122   M. A. BUFORD

Table 8.1   (continued)

Item no	Item	Concept	Source
17	When communicating with my direct supervisor, I favor partnering with others to try to change their point of view, particularly when they are wrong	Speak in	Yulk (2010)
18	When my organization is confronted with an ethical dilemma, the best course of action to help my leader to change is to create organizational allies	Speak in	Yulk (2010)
19	When different respected followers convey the same message to my leader, it can sway them to do the right thing	Speak in	Yulk (2010)
20	If my leader directs me to accomplish an unprincipled mission, I would use a team of fellow followers to convince them to rescind the order	Speak in	Yulk (2010)
21	When communicating with my direct supervisor, it is important to me to stand on right principles to try to change their point of view	Speak in	I Chr 21:9–12
22	When my organization is confronted with an ethical dilemma, the best course of action to help my leader to change is with a values-centric, direct approach	Speak in	I Chr 21:9–12
23	If a person in the organization with a strong values-based reputation approached my leader, it can sway them to do the right thing	Speak in	I Chr 21:9–12
24	If my leader directs me to accomplish an unprincipled mission, approaching them privately while standing on what is right can convince them to rescind the order	Speak in	I Chr 21:9–12
25	When I feel powerless in an unethical organization, I find myself using cynical conversations to make myself feel better	Speak out	Num 16
26	Unethical orders should be accomplished pessimistically	Speak out	Num 16
27	It is an acceptable organizational practice to insert negativity into the job as the team performs an unethical order	Speak out	Num 16
28	If given the opportunity to champion an unethical order from a leader I respect, I would execute it and complain to everyone along the way	Speak out	Num 16
29	When I feel powerless in an immoral organization, I have no problem leaking information to different outlets to expose the problem	Speak out	Chenoweth and Stephan (2011)

(*continued*)

MEASURING YOUR ORGANIZATION'S BOARDROOM LANGUAGE   123

Table 8.1   (continued)

Item no	Item	Concept	Source
30	Unethical orders should be reported to the media to resolve the issue	Speak out	Chenoweth and Stephan (2011)
31	It is my duty to call an anonymous hotline to stop an unethical order or practice	Speak out	Chenoweth and Stephan (2011)
32	If given the opportunity to execute an unethical order from a leader I respect, I would demonstrate my loyalty to the organization by secretly reporting it	Speak out	Chenoweth and Stephan (2011)
33	When I feel powerless in an unprincipled organization, I have no problem speaking out in a public and nonviolent manner	Speak out	Engler and Engler (2016)
34	Unethical orders should be resisted with the tool of striking	Speak out	Engler and Engler (2016)
35	It is my duty to join fellow organizational protesters to stop an unethical order or practice	Speak out	Engler and Engler (2016)
36	If given the opportunity to execute an unethical order from a leader I respect, I would demonstrate my loyalty to the organization by protesting in a public way	Speak out	Engler and Engler (2016)
37	If I worked in an unethical organization, resisting flawed practices until fired is an honorable gesture	Step down	Gordon (2012)
38	Unethical orders should be resisted, even if it leads to being fired	Step down	Gordon (2012)
39	It is my duty to resist until being fired to stop an unethical order or practice	Step down	Gordon (2012)
40	If given the opportunity to execute an unethical order from a leader I respect, I would demonstrate my loyalty to the organization by resisting until being fired	Step down	Gordon (2012)
41	If I were employed by an institution that suddenly adopted an immoral policy, retirement is an appropriate tool to convey a principled message	Step down	Felice (2009)
42	Unethical orders should be resisted by retiring if I had tenure	Step down	Felice (2009)
43	It is my duty to send a message by retiring if I had tenure to stop an unethical order or practice	Step down	Felice (2009)
44	If given the opportunity to execute an unethical order from a leader I respect, I would retire to send a message and show my loyalty to the organization	Step down	Felice (2009)

(*continued*)

124 M. A. BUFORD

Table 8.1 (continued)

Item no	Item	Concept	Source
45	If I were employed by an institution that suddenly adopted an immoral policy, a letter of resignation is an appropriate tool to convey a moral message	Step down	Felice (2009)
46	Unethical orders should be resisted by resigning	Step down	Felice (2009)
47	It is my duty to send a message by resigning to protest an unethical order or practice	Step down	I Chr 21:16–17
48	If given the opportunity to execute an unethical order from a leader I respect, I would resign to send a message and show my loyalty to the organization	Step down	I Chr 21:16–17
49	If a leader implements an immoral policy, I will exercise the moral fortitude to turn things around	Step it up	Ex 17:11–13
50	It is my belief that followers of this organization are on one accord, work with urgency, embrace prayer as tool for change and are proactive	Step it up	Ex 17:11–13
51	My executive leader is willing to accept responsibility for wrong actions, listens actively, is a lifelong learning, and empowers the team to accomplish the mission	Step it up	Ex 17:11–13

Table 8.2 Age

		Frequency	Percent	Valid percent	Cumulative percent
Valid	18–29	96	37.5	37.5	37.5
	30–44	90	35.2	35.2	72.7
	45–60	33	12.9	12.9	85.5
	>60	37	14.5	14.5	100.0
	Total	256	100.0	100.0	

Table 8.3 Gender

		Frequency	Percent	Valid percent	Cumulative percent
Valid	Male	84	32.8	32.8	32.8
	Female	172	67.2	67.2	100.0
	Total	256	100.0	100.0	

Therefore, this process attempted to gage the most advantageous way to measure the intangibles of boardroom language as delineated in this book to create a scale that evaluated an organizational citizen's propensity to:

1. Shut up—To instantaneously and silently obey orders.
2. Speak in—The ability to utilize truth as a tool to transform a leader's paradigm and their toxic behavior.
3. Speak out—The utilization of peaceful and purposeful means to adjudicate a wrong in a public manner.
4. Step down—The ability of a leader to remove themselves for the health of the organization as well as themselves.
5. Step it up—The ability of the organizational citizen to proactively act to heal and transform the culture.

STEP 2: GENERATE AN ITEM POOL

DeVellis contends that the second step of scale development is to generate an item pool and offers several practical recommendations, which include: (a) devise a large pool of items; (b) utilize language that is easy for a reading level between the fifth and seventh grades (this is the level for newspapers); and (c) write positively worded items.[3] Taking account of DeVillis' insights, Table 8.1 shows the initial item pool for the five scales.

Table 8.4 Income

		Frequency	Percent	Valid percent	Cumulative percent
Valid	$0–$9999	36	14.1	14.1	14.1
	$10,000–$24,999	25	9.8	9.8	23.8
	$25,000–$49,999	59	23.0	23.0	46.9
	$50,000–$74,999	39	15.2	15.2	62.1
	$75,000–$99,999	38	14.8	14.8	77.0
	$100,000–$124,999	14	5.5	5.5	82.4
	$125,000–$149,999	4	1.6	1.6	84.0
	$150,000–$174,999	7	2.7	2.7	86.7
	$175,000–$199,999	4	1.6	1.6	88.3
	$200,000+	6	2.3	2.3	90.6
	Prefer not to answer	24	9.4	9.4	100.0
	Total	256	100.0	100.0	

[3] Ibid.

Step 3: Determine the Format for Measurement

The third step of scale development is to establish the format for measurement. Although DeVellis suggests that steps two and three are related, he stresses that careful consideration should be given to the format. Thus, this endeavor proposed utilizing a seven-item Likert design. DeVellis indicates that "a good Likert item should state the opinion, attitude, belief, or other construct under study in clear terms."[4] As such, the following composition guided the items.

1	–	7
Not at all		All the time

Step 4: Have the Initial Item Pool Reviewed by Experts

The fourth step of scale development is to have the original item pool reviewed by a panel of experts. DeVellis defines an expert as "colleagues who have worked extensively with the construct in question or related phenomena."[5] The panel for this study consisted of five scholars with a strong command of instrument development. Their task, as delineated by DeVellis, was multifaceted and included:

1. Confirm or invalidate the selected definitions of the phenomenon. More specifically, the experts were asked to rate online how relevant they thought each item was with regards to measuring the various phenomena (1 = very relevant, 2 = somewhat relevant, 3 = neutral, 4 = related to the concept, 5 = very related to the concept).
2. Comment freely on individual items for improvement.
3. Evaluate each item's clarity and conciseness.
4. Point out additional ways to tap into the phenomena that the researcher may have failed to include.
5. In addition to rating the items, the major feedback from the panel was included.

---

[4] Ibid. p. 80.
[5] Ibid. p. 86.

STEP 5: CONSIDER INCLUSION OF VALIDATION ITEMS

The fifth step of scale development revolved around the inclusion of validated items. To this end, a decision was made to include all items that received a rating of neutral or better from the panel of scholars. This process discarded item 47 due to redundancy and wording.

STEP 6: ADMINISTER ITEMS TO A DEVELOPMENT SAMPLE

The sixth step of a scale development as prescribed by DeVellis is to administer the scale to a sample. There is much debate on what constitutes an adequate number for a sample size. Nummally and Bernstein contend that the sample should include at least 300 people, since such a figure will proactively defuse the unstable factor regarding patterns of covariation among the myriad items.[6] Whereas, DeVellis suggests that 5–10 participants per item is acceptable. To this end, the sample size peaked at 340.

A web-based company was utilized to help randomly solicit participants who were informed that they were invited to take a survey that would take approximately 10–15 minutes to complete, and that their participation would help to understand a follower's propensity better to speak out or to obey an unethical order. The survey was available to those with access to the Internet and who lived in the United States. The participants understood that if they did not feel comfortable completing the confidential survey, they could opt out at any time.

STEP 7: EVALUATE THE ITEMS

DeVellis suggests that the seventh step of scale development is to evaluate the items. The primary intent of item analysis is to identify entries that form a consistent internal scale and to eliminate other items. This study adhered to such guidance by employing version 25 of the Statistical Package for Social Scientists (SPSS) to understand if there were one or more scales affiliated with the five concepts of this book. First, a decision was made to remove items that were either incomplete or contained flawed data. Although 340 participants initially engaged in the study, 84 entries were discarded, which reduced the sample size to 256. It should be noted that the new sample size, N = 256, remained within DeVellis' five per item guidance and is therefore adequate for scale development.

[6]Nunnally, Jum C., and Ira H. Bernstein. 1978. *Psychometric Theory.* USA: McGraw-Hill.

128 M. A. BUFORD

Table 8.5 Region

		Frequency	Percent	Valid percent	Cumulative percent
Valid	New England	22	8.6	8.6	8.6
	Middle Atlantic	27	10.5	10.5	19.1
	East North Central	30	11.7	11.7	30.9
	West North Central	9	3.5	3.5	34.4
	South Atlantic	56	21.9	21.9	56.3
	East South Central	17	6.6	6.6	62.9
	West South Central	25	9.8	9.8	72.7
	Mountain	33	12.9	12.9	85.5
	Pacific	37	14.5	14.5	100.0
	Total	256	100.0	100.0	

The demographics of the sample as depicted in Tables 8.2, 8.3, 8.4, and 8.5 was 37.5 percent between the ages of 18–29, 35.2 percent were 30–44, 12.9 percent were 45–60 and 14.5 percent were 60 or older. There were 67.2 percent female and 32.8 percent male, with a household income that ranged from \$0–\$9999 to \$200,000+. The sample were located across the USA, 8.6 percent of the sample were from New England, 10.5 percent from the Middle Atlantic, 11.7 percent from the East North Central, 3.5 percent from the West North Central, 21.9 percent from the South Atlantic, 6.6 percent from the East South Central, 9.8 percent from the West South Central, 12.9 percent from the Mountain and 14.5 percent were from the Pacific region. Ethnic demographics were not collected in the survey.

Data Analysis of the Shut-Up Concept

SPSS version 25 was employed to perform an analysis of the data. Specifically, Pearson correlation was applied to items SU1, SU2, SU3, SU4, SU5, SU6, SU7, SU8, SU9, SU10, SU11 and SU12 (see Table 8.1) to measure the degree of linear relationship between two or more variables.

As depicted in Table 8.6, there was evidence of a positive relationship between the variables at the 0.01 level (one-tailed) and the 0.05 level (two-tailed). Hair et al. contend that the correlated variables suggest the direct oblique rotation solution is appropriate for exploratory factor analysis in such a case. Moreover, the literature suggests that items that load at 0.40 or above are acceptable in factor analysis.[7] To this end, loadings that fail under this threshold were suppressed.

[7] Hair, Joseph F, William C Black, Barry J Babin, and Rolph E Anderson. 2003. *Multivariate Data Analysis.* Upper Saddle River: Prentice Hall.

Table 8.6 Shut-up correlation matrix

Item	SU1	SU2	SU3	SU4	SU5	SU6	SU7	SU8	SU9	SU10	SU11	SU12
SU1	1.00											
SU2	0.81**	1.00										
SU3	0.71**	0.73**	1.00									
SU4	0.75**	0.75**	0.74**	1.00								
SU5	0.41**	0.40**	0.29**	0.43**	1.00							
SU6	0.41**	0.39**	0.34**	0.43**	0.69**	1.00						
SU7	0.69**	0.74**	0.61**	0.72**	0.42**	0.32**	1.00					
SU8	0.69**	0.62**	0.50**	0.61**	0.53**	0.41**	0.75**	1.00				
SU9	0.13*	0.19**	00.9	0.15*	0.40**	0.35**	0.19**	0.24**	1.00			
SU10	0.12*	0.15*	0.08	0.15*	0.37**	0.35**	0.15*	0.23**	0.78**	1.00		
SU11	0.05	0.13*	0.08	0.13*	0.27**	0.29**	0.08	0.10	0.61**	0.69**	1.00	
SU12	−0.12*	−0.08	−0.09	−0.08	0.19**	0.19**	−0.13*	−0.06	0.41**	0.51**	0.63**	1.00

*Correlation is significant at the 0.05 level (2-tailed)
**Correlation is significant at the 0.01 level (2-tailed)

The Kaiser-Meyer-Olkin (KMO) test and the Bartlett test of sphericity were conducted. KMO accesses how suitable data is for factor analysis, and measures sampling adequacy for each variable in the model. Additionally, the KMO measures the proportion of variance among variables that might be common variance.[8] The value returns of the KMO range from 0 to 1. Kaiser provides the following rule of thumb for the values returned (0.00–0.49 unacceptable, 0.50–0.59 miserable, 0.60–0.69 mediocre, 0.70–0.79 middling, 0.80–0.89 meritorious and 0.90–1.00 marvelous).[9] The KMO returned a value of 0.860. The Bartlett test of sphericity is "a statistical test for the presence of correlations among variables... It provides statistical significance that the correlation matrix has significant correlations among at least some of the variables."[10] Thus, the KMO and the p-value that registered at 0.000 suggest there was enough evidence to conduct a factor analysis.

A principle component analysis was conducted on items SU1–SU12. O'Rourke and Hatcher posited that the best method to understand oblique rotation is to, "always review the pattern matrix to determine which groups of variables are measuring a given factor, for purposes of interpreting the meaning of that factor."[11] To this end, a pattern matrix was generated and two factors for the shut-up concept were identified. The analysis also identified cross-loadings on items SU5 and SU6. Hair et al. maintain that when a variable is found to have more than one significant loading, it becomes a candidate for deletion.[12] As such, these items were deleted, and a component analysis was employed on the remaining ten items.

An interpretation of Table 8.7 reveals no additional cross-loadings and the existence of two factors. Component 1 factored items SU1, SU2, SU3, SU4, SU7 and SU8 that were labeled *shut-up and comply*. Component 2 was comprised of items SU9, SU10, SU11, and SU12 that were labeled *shut-up and sabotage* as depicted in Table 8.9. A reliability analysis was conducted that produced a Cronbach's alpha, which "is a single correlation coefficient that is an estimate of the average of all the correlation coefficients of the items within a test. If alpha is high (0.80 or higher), then this suggests that all the items are

[8] Glen, Stephanie. 2016. "Kaiser-Meyer-Olkin (KMO) Test for Sampling Adequacy." *How to Statistics*. May 11. Accessed December 23, 2017. http://www.statisticshowto.com/kaiser-meyer-olkin/

[9] Kaiser, H. 1974. "An index of factor simplicity." *Psychometrika* 39: 31–36.

[10] Hair, Joseph F, William C Black, Barry J Babin, and Rolph E Anderson. 2003. *Multivariate Data Analysis*. Upper Saddle River: Prentice Hall. p. 104.

[11] O'Rourke, Norm, and Larry Hatcher. 2013. *A Step-by-Step Approach to Using SAS for Factor Analysis and Structural Equation Modeling 2nd Edition*. North Carolina: SAS Institute Inc. p. 72.

[12] Ibid.

MEASURING YOUR ORGANIZATION'S BOARDROOM LANGUAGE **131**

Table 8.7 Regenerated shut-up pattern matrix

	Component	
	1	*2*
SU1 Leader unethical order 101 percent effort mission	0.903	
SU2 Unethical orders extraordinary effort	0.897	
SU3 Duty to not only comply unethical order one step beyond	0.830	
SU4 Champion unethical order respected leader	0.879	
SU7 Duty to comply with an immoral order	0.871	
SU8 Immoral order from a leader I respect nothing more	0.794	
SU9 Leader secretly try to sabotage it innovately		0.824
SU10 Unprincipled orders sabotaged with creative energy		0.884
SU11 Duty to not only disrupt an unprincipled order		0.873
SU12 Unprincipled order best imaginative option to stop it		0.769

Table 8.8 Shut-up and comply scale

Item no	*Item*
SU3	It is my duty to not only comply with an unethical order but to go one step beyond it
SU4	If given the opportunity to champion an unethical order from a leader I respect, I will gladly execute it and go one step further
SU7	It is my duty to comply with an immoral order
SU8	If given the opportunity to comply with an immoral order from a leader I respect, I will execute it and do nothing more

reliable, and the entire test is internally consistent."[13] To this end, Cronbach's alpha with no alterations for *shut-up and comply* rendered a score of 0.93 with N = 6. DeVellis asserts, however, that the last step in scale development is to maximize the scale length. Once the item reliability has been established, DeVellis posited that a researcher should spend time thinking about brevity, "when the researcher has 'reliability to spare,' it may be appropriate to buy a shorter scale at the price of a little less reliability."[14] As such, the item-total statistic matrix was inspected, and several items were recommended for

---

[13] Ho, Robert. 2006. *Handbook of Univariate and Multivariate Data Analysis and Interpretation with SPSS.* New York: Chapman & Hall/CRC. p. 240.

[14] DeVellis, Robert F. 2017. *Scale Development Theory and Applications.* London: Sage Publications. p. 146.

132   M. A. BUFORD

Table 8.9   Shut-up and sabotage scale

Item no	Item
SU9	If my leader directs me to accomplish an unprincipled mission, I will secretly try to sabotage it innovately
SU10	Unprincipled orders should be sabotaged with creative energy
SU11	It is my duty to not only disrupt an unprincipled order but to also undermine it in a unique manner
SU12	If given the opportunity to interrupt an unprincipled order from a leader I respect, I would use my best imaginative option to stop it

removal. More specifically, it was found that the deleted αs were the same for two items—SU1 and SU2, which were removed—and the renewed Cronbach alpha for *shut-up and comply* became 0.88 with N = 4. Cronbach's alpha with no alterations rendered a score of 0.86 with N = 4 for *Shut-up and sabotage*. While Cronbach's alpha for *shut-up and sabotage* could be improved slightly, a decision was made not to remove an article so that both factors had four items.

Data Analysis of the Speak-In Concept

SPSS version 25 was employed to perform an analysis of the *speak-in* concept. Specifically, Pearson correlation was applied to items SI13, SI14, SI15, SI16, SI17, SI18, SI19, SI20, SI21, SI22, SI23 and SI24 with the intent to measure the degree of linear relationship between two or more variables.

As depicted in Table 8.10, this process revealed that there was evidence of a positive relationship between the variables at the 0.01 level (two-tailed). Hair et al. contend the correlated variables suggest that the direct oblique rotation solution is appropriate for exploratory factor analysis in such a case. Moreover, the literature suggests that items that load at 0.40 or above are acceptable in factor analysis.[15] To this end, loadings that fail under this threshold were suppressed.

The KMO test and the Bartlett test of sphericity were conducted. The KMO returned a value of 0.89 and the p-value registered at 0.000 which suggest there was enough evidence to conduct a factor analysis.

---

[15] Hair, Joseph F, William C Black, Barry J Babin, and Rolph E Anderson. 2003. *Multivariate Data Analysis*. Upper Saddle River: Prentice Hall.

MEASURING YOUR ORGANIZATION'S BOARDROOM LANGUAGE   133

Table 8.13 Speak-in correlation matrix

Item	SI13	SI14	SI15	SI16	SI17	SI18	SI19	SI20	SI21	SI22	SI23	SI24
SI13	1.00											
SI14	0.60**	1.00										
SI15	0.50**	0.58**	1.00									
SI16	0.49**	0.51**	0.70**	1.00								
SI17	0.52**	0.48**	0.52**	0.58**	1.00							
SI18	0.49**	0.45**	0.48**	0.54**	0.62**	1.00						
SI19	0.42**	0.48**	0.67**	0.61**	0.56**	0.61**	1.00					
SI20	0.47**	0.43**	0.48**	0.54**	0.72**	0.63**	0.59**	1.00				
SI21	0.32**	0.21**	0.36**	0.45**	0.33**	0.29**	0.38**	0.39**	1.00			
SI22	0.24**	0.24**	0.36**	0.37**	0.24**	0.29**	0.34**	0.38**	0.64**	1.00		
SI23	0.22**	0.25**	0.46**	0.44**	0.28**	0.28**	0.43**	0.37**	0.54**	0.66**	1.00	
SI24	0.28**	0.33**	0.45**	0.41**	0.24**	0.29**	0.36**	0.31**	0.39**	0.51**	0.57**	1.00

**Correlation is significant at the 0.01 level (2-tailed)

bListwise N = 256

Table 8.11 Speak-in pattern matrix

	Component	
	1	*2*
SI13 Stories when they are wrong	0.770	
SI14 Change is with an appropriate story	0.771	
SI15 Historical narrative moral decision	0.677	
SI16 Unprincipled mission values-based story	0.684	
SI17 Partnering others to change their point of view	0.865	
SI18 Create organizational allies	0.809	
SI19 Different respected followers sway	0.712	
SI20 A team of fellow followers rescind the order	0.741	
SI21 Stand on right principles		0.748
SI22 A values-based direct approach		0.898
SI23 A strong values-based reputation		0.866
SI24 Approaching them privately		0.699

Extraction method: principal component analysis
Rotation method: Oblimin with Kaiser normalization
[a]Rotation converged in 4 iterations

A principle component analysis was conducted on items SI13–SI24. O'Rourke and Hatcher posited that the best method to understand oblique rotation is to, "always review the pattern matrix to determine which groups of variables are measuring a given factor, for purposes of interpreting the meaning of that factor."[16] To this end, a pattern matrix was generated and two factors for the speak-in concept identified. As depicted in Table 8.11, component 1 factored items SI13, SI14, SI15, S16, SI17, SI18, SI19 and SI20 that were labeled *speak-in with a parable*. Component 2 was comprised of items SI21, SI22, SI23 and SI24 that were labeled *speak-in on principles*. A reliability analysis was conducted on *speak-in with a parable* that produced a Cronbach's alpha score of 0.90 with N = 8. DeVellis again asserts that "when the researcher has 'reliability to spare,' it may be appropriate to buy a shorter scale at the price of a little less reliability."[17] As such, the item-total statistic matrix was inspected, and several items were recommended for removal. A decision was made to remove those items with the lowest αs. Hence, items SI16, SI17, SI19,

[16]O'Rourke, Norm, and Larry Hatcher. 2013. *A Step-by-Step Approach to Using SAS for Factor Analysis and Structural Equation Modeling 2nd Edition*. North Carolina: SAS Institute Inc. p. 72.

[17]DeVellis, Robert F. 2017. *Scale Development Theory and Applications*. London: Sage Publications. p. 146.

MEASURING YOUR ORGANIZATION'S BOARDROOM LANGUAGE   135

Table 8.12   Speak-in with a parable scale

Item no	Item
SI13	When communicating with my direct supervisor, I prefer to use stories to try to change their point of view particularly when they are wrong
SI14	When my organization is confronted with an ethical dilemma, the best course of action to help my leader to change is with an appropriate story
SI15	When a relevant historical narrative is provided to my leader, it can help them to make a moral decision
SI18	When my organization is confronted with an ethical dilemma, the best course of action to help my leader to change is to create organizational allies

Table 8.13   Speak-in on principles

Item no	Item
SI21	When communicating with my direct supervisor, it is important to me to stand on right principles to try to change their point of view
SI22	When my organization is confronted with an ethical dilemma, the best course of action to help my leader to change is with a values centric direct approach
SI23	If a person in the organization with a strong values-based reputation approached my leader, it can sway them to do the right thing
SI24	If my leader directs me to accomplish an unprincipled mission, approaching them privately while standing on what is right can convince them to rescind the order

and SI20 were removed and the renewed Cronbach's alpha for *speak-in with a parable* decreased to 0.81 with N = 4. Cronbach's alpha rendered a score of 0.82 with N = 4 for *speak-in on principles*. An examination of the item-total statistic matrix showed that the removal of additional items would not improve α for *speak-in on principles*.

Data Analysis of the Speak-Out Concept

SPSS version 25 was employed to perform an analysis of the *speak-out concept*. Specifically, Pearson correlation was applied to items SO25, SO26, SO27, SO28, SO29, SO30, SO31, SO32, SO33, S034, SO35 and SO36 with the intent to measure the degree of linear relationship between two or more variables.

Table 8.14 showed there was evidence of a positive relationship between the variables at the 0.01 level (two-tailed). Hair et al. contend the correlated variables suggest that the direct oblique rotation solution is appropriate for exploratory factor analysis in such a case. Additionally, the

Table 8.14 Speak-out correlation matrix

Item	SO25	SO26	SO27	SO28	SO29	SO30	SO31	SO32	SO33	SO34	SO35	SO36
SO25	1.00											
SO26	0.34**	1.00										
SO27	0.42**	0.48**	1.00									
SO28	0.48**	0.49**	0.54**	1.00								
SO29	0.38**	0.30**	0.49**	0.37**	1.00							
SO30	0.32**	0.38**	0.42**	0.43**	0.60**	1.00						
SO31	0.10	0.04	0.18**	0.10	0.28**	0.20**	1.00					
SO32	0.12	0.30**	0.32**	0.23**	0.32**	0.39**	0.55**	1.00				
SO33	0.11	0.20**	0.26**	0.22**	0.40**	0.47**	0.31**	0.40**	1.00			
SO34	0.31**	0.27**	0.39**	0.29**	0.46**	0.48**	0.35**	0.25**	0.39**	1.00		
SO35	0.19**	0.08	0.21**	0.18**	0.35**	0.34**	0.39**	0.24**	0.43**	0.58**	1.00	
SO36	0.26**	0.28**	0.37**	0.32**	0.48**	0.57**	0.38**	0.46**	0.60**	0.64**	0.61**	1.00

**Correlation is significant at the 0.01 level (2-tailed)

[b]Listwise N = 256

literature suggests that items that load at 0.40 or above are acceptable in factor analysis.[18] In a similar vein as the *shut-up* and *speak-in* concepts, loadings that failed under this threshold were suppressed.

The KMO test and Bartlett test of sphericity were conducted. The KMO returned a value of 0.85 and the p-value registered at 0.000, which suggested there was enough evidence to conduct a factor analysis.

A principle component analysis was conducted on items SO25–SO36. O'Rourke and Hatcher posited that the best method to understand oblique rotation is to, "always review the pattern matrix to determine which groups of variables are measuring a given factor, for purposes of interpreting the meaning of that factor."[19] To this end, a pattern matrix was generated and two factors for the speak-out concept identified. Moreover, the analysis also identified cross-loadings on items SO29 and SO30. Hair et al. maintain that when a variable is found to have more than one significant loading, it becomes a candidate for deletion.[20] To this end, these items were deleted, and a component analysis was employed on the remaining ten items.

As depicted in Table 8.15, component 1 factored items SO31, SO32, SO33, SO34, SO35, and SO36 that were labeled *speak-out nonviolently*. A

Table 8.15 Speak-out pattern matrix

	Component	
	1	*2*
SO25 Cynical conversations		0.713
SO26 Unethical orders accomplished pessimistically		0.769
SO27 Insert negativity performs an unethical order		0.739
SO28 Complain along the way		0.821
SO31 Anonymous hotline unethical order	0.746	
SO32 Respect loyalty secretly reporting	0.606	
SO33 Speaking out nonviolent manner	0.704	
SO34 Unethical orders resisted striking	0.658	
SO35 Join protesters stop unethical practice	0.788	
SO36 Protesting in a public way	0.796	

Extraction method: principal component analysis
Rotation method: Oblimin with Kaiser normalization

ᵃRotation converged in four iterations

[18] Hair, Joseph F, William C Black, Barry J Babin, and Rolph E Anderson. 2003. *Multivariate Data Analysis*. Upper Saddle River: Prentice Hall.
[19] O'Rourke, Norm, and Larry Hatcher. 2013. *A Step-by-Step Approach to Using SAS for Factor Analysis and Structural Equation Modeling 2nd Edition*. North Carolina: SAS Institute Inc. p. 72.
[20] Ibid.

138 M. A. BUFORD

Table 8.16 Speak-out nonviolently scale

Item no	Item
SO33	When I feel powerless in an unprincipled organization, I have no problem speaking out in a public and nonviolent manner
SO34	Unethical orders should be resisted with the tool of striking
SO35	It is my duty to join fellow organizational protesters to stop an unethical order or practice
SO36	If given the opportunity to execute an unethical order from a leader I respect, I would demonstrate my loyalty to the organization by protesting in a public way

Table 8.17 Speak-out negatively scale

Item no	Item
SO25	When I feel powerless in an unethical organization, I find myself using cynical conversations to make myself feel better
SO26	Unethical orders should be accomplished pessimistically
SO27	It is an acceptable organizational practice to insert negativity into the job as the team performs an unethical order
SO28	If given the opportunity to champion an unethical order from a leader I respect, I would execute it and complain to everyone along the way

reliability analysis was conducted on *speak-out nonviolently* that produced a Cronbach's alpha score of 0.82 with N = 6. An examination of the item-total statistic matrix showed that the removal of additional items would not improve α. However, DeVellis posited that a researcher should spend time thinking about brevity.[21] To this end, an analysis of the item-total statistic matrix revealed that the removal of items with the lowest scores, SO31 and SO32, would not negatively impact α. Once Cronbach's alpha was recalculated, the score remained at 0.82 with N = 4. Component 2 was comprised of items SO25, SO26, SO27 and SO28 that were labeled *speak-out negatively*. A reliability analysis was conducted on *speak-out negatively* that produced a Cronbach's alpha score of 0.77 with N = 4. An inspection of the item-total statistic matrix showed that the removal of additional items would not improve α.

[21]DeVellis, Robert F. 2017. *Scale Development Theory and Applications*. London: Sage Publications. p. 146.

Data Analysis of the Step-Down Concept

SPSS version 25 was employed to perform an analysis of the *step-down concept*. Specifically, Pearson correlation was applied to items SD37, SD38, SD39, SD40, SD41, SD42, SD43, SD44, SD45, SD46, and SD47 with the intent to measure the degree of linear relationship between two or more variables.

Table 8.18 showed that there was evidence of a positive relationship between the variables at the 0.01 level (two-tailed). Hair et al. contend the correlated variables suggest that the direct oblique rotation solution is appropriate for exploratory factor analysis in such a case. Moreover, the literature suggests that items that load at 0.40 or above are acceptable in factor analysis.[22] In keeping with the other concepts, loadings that fail under this threshold were suppressed.

The KMO test and Bartlett test of sphericity were conducted. The KMO returned a value of 0.85 and the p-value registered at 0.000 which suggest there was enough evidence to conduct a factor analysis.

A principle component analysis was conducted on items SD37–SD47. O'Rourke and Hatcher posited that the best method to understand oblique rotation is to, "always review the pattern matrix to determine which groups of variables are measuring a given factor, for purposes of interpreting the meaning of that factor."[23] To this end, a pattern matrix was generated, and two factors for the step-down concept were identified.

As depicted in Table 8.19, component 1 factored items SD41, SD42, SD43, SD44, SD45, SD46 and SD47 which were labeled *step-down by resigning*. A reliability analysis was conducted on *step-down by resigning* that produced a Cronbach's alpha score of 0.91 with N = 7.

As alluded to before, DeVellis contends that "when the researcher has 'reliability to spare,' it may be appropriate to buy a shorter scale at the price of a little less reliability."[24] Thus, the item-total statistic matrix was inspected, and several items were recommended for removal. A decision was made to remove the three items with the lowest α's—SD42, SD44 and SD47. Once these items were removed, a Cronbach's alpha for *step-down by resigning*

---

[22] Hair, Joseph F, William C Black, Barry J Babin, and Rolph E Anderson. 2003. *Multivariate Data Analysis*. Upper Saddle River: Prentice Hall.

[23] O'Rourke, Norm, and Larry Hatcher. 2013. *A Step by Step Approach to Using SAS for Factor Analysis and Structural Equation Modeling 2nd Edition*. North Carolina: SAS Institute Inc. p. 72.

[24] DeVellis, Robert F. 2017. *Scale Development Theory and Applications*. London: Sage Publications. p. 146.

Table 8.18 Step-down correlation matrix

Item	SD37	SD38	SD39	SD40	SD41	SD42	SD43	SD44	SD45	SD46	SD47
SD37	1.00										
SD38	0.55**	1.00									
SD39	0.64**	0.83**	1.00								
SD40	0.55**	0.70**	0.69**	1.00							
SD41	0.24**	0.36**	0.33**	0.39**	1.00						
SD42	0.43**	0.41**	0.42**	0.38**	0.70**	1.00					
SD43	0.32**	0.23**	0.31**	0.35**	0.58**	0.74**	1.00				
SD44	0.30**	0.41**	0.37**	0.43**	0.75**	0.72**	0.66**	1.00			
SD45	0.38**	0.48**	0.51**	0.53**	0.50**	0.48**	0.55**	0.53**	1.00		
SD46	0.35**	0.50**	0.48**	0.35**	0.52**	0.56**	0.32**	0.64**	0.53**	1.00	
SD47	0.33**	0.44**	0.45**	0.50**	0.51**	0.56**	0.55**	0.65**	0.71**	0.66**	1.00

**Correlation is significant at the 0.01 level (2-tailed)

[b]Listwise N = 256

MEASURING YOUR ORGANIZATION'S BOARDROOM LANGUAGE   141

Table 8.19   Step-down pattern matrix

	Component	
	1	*2*
SD37 Resisting until fired		0.773
SD38 Resisted even if it leads to being fired		0.900
SD39 Duty to resist until fired		0.930
SD40 Leader respect resisting until being fired		0.796
SD41 Retirement is an appropriate principled message	0.878	
SD42 Retiring if I had the tenure	0.855	
SD43 Duty retiring stop unethical order or practice	0.873	
SD44 Leader respect retire	0.909	
SD45 A letter of resignation	0.553	
SD46 Resist by resigning	0.581	
SD47 Leader I respect resign loyalty to the organization	0.691	

Extraction method: principal component analysis
Rotation method: Oblimin with Kaiser normalization
[a]Rotation converged in five iterations

Table 8.20   Step-down by resigning scale

item no	Item
SD41	If I were employed by an institution that suddenly adopted an immoral policy, retirement is an appropriate tool to convey a principled message
SD43	It is my duty to send a message by retiring if I had the tenure to stop an unethical order or practice
SD45	If I were employed by an institution that suddenly adopted an immoral policy, a letter of resignation is an appropriate tool to convey a moral message
SD46	Unethical orders should be resisted by resigning

Table 8.21   Step-down by resisting scale

Item no	Item
SD37	If I worked in an unethical organization, resisting flawed practices until fired is an honorable gesture
SD38	Unethical orders should be resisted even if it leads to being fired
SD39	It is my duty to resist until being fired to stop an unethical order or practice
SD40	If given the opportunity to execute an unethical order from a leader I respect, I would demonstrate my loyalty to the organization by resisting until being fired

142   M. A. BUFORD

regenerated a score of 0.79 with N = 4. Component 2 was comprised of items SD37, SD38, SD39 and SD40 that were labeled *step-down by resisting*. A reliability analysis was conducted on *step-down by resisting* that produced a Cronbach's alpha score of 0.88 with N = 4. Although Cronbach's alpha for *step-down by resisting* could be improved slightly, a decision was made not to remove an item for the sake of factor consistency.

Data Analysis of the Step-It-Up Concept

SPSS version 25 was employed to perform an analysis of the *step-it-up concept*. Specifically, Pearson correlation was applied to items SIU48, SIU49, and SIU50 with the intent to measure the degree of linear relationship between two or more variables.

Table 8.22 showed that there was evidence of a positive relationship between the variables at the 0.01 level (two-tailed). Hair et al. contend the correlated variables suggest that the direct oblique rotation solution is appropriate for exploratory factor analysis in such a case. Moreover, the literature suggests that items that load at 0.40 or above are acceptable in factor analysis.[25] In keeping with the other concepts, loadings that fail under this threshold were suppressed.

The KMO test and Bartlett test of sphericity were conducted. The KMO returned a value of 0.67 and the p-value registered at 0.000 which suggest there was enough evidence to conduct a factor analysis.

A principle component analysis was conducted on items SIU48–SIU50. O'Rourke and Hatcher posited that the best method to understand oblique

Table 8.22   Step-it-up correlation matrix

Item	SIU48	SIU49	SIU50
SIU48	1.00		
SIU49	0.50**	1.00	
SIU50	0.45**	0.45**	1.00

**Correlation is significant at the 0.01 level (2-tailed)
[b]Listwise N = 256

[25] Hair, Joseph F, William C Black, Barry J Babin, and Rolph E Anderson. 2003. *Multivariate Data Analysis*. Upper Saddle River: Prentice Hall.

rotation is to, "always review the pattern matrix to determine which groups of variables are measuring a given factor, for purposes of interpreting the meaning of that factor."[26] To this end, a pattern matrix was generated, and two factors for the step-down concept were identified.

As depicted in Table 8.23, component 1 factored items SIU48 and SIU49 that were labeled *step-it-up morally*. Component 2 factored item SIU50 that were labeled *step-it-out with reflective leadership*. *Step-it-up morally* and *step-it-out with reflective leadership* were deemed empirically unsuitable for scale development because there were two items or fewer in the components.[27] Thus, no further analysis was warranted for the *step-it-up* concept.

STEP 8: OPTIMIZE SCALE LENGTH

The last step in scale development according to DeVellis is to optimize the scale length. Once the item reliability has been established, DeVellis' guidance that a researcher should spend time thinking about brevity was followed. Although shortness of the scales may potentially threaten reliability, it may also increase the probability of participation due to time constraints. This point may particularly resonate within today's high-paced culture. Upon removal of the "bad" items as driven by statistical

Table 8.23 Step-it-up pattern matrix

	Component	
	1	2
SIU 48 Moral fortitude turn things around	0.864	
SIU 49 One accord urgency prayer proactive	0.869	
SIU 50 Responsibility listens actively lifelong learner empowers		1.000

Extraction method: principal component analysis
Rotation method: Oblimin with Kaiser normalization

ªRotation converged in three iterations

[26] O'Rourke, Norm, and Larry Hatcher. 2013. *A Step-by-Step Approach to Using SAS for Factor Analysis and Structural Equation Modeling 2nd Edition*. North Carolina: SAS Institute Inc. p. 72.

[27] Raubenheimer, J. E. 2004. "An item selection procedure to maximize scale reliabilty and validity." *South African Journal of Industial Psychology, Vol 30 No 4* 59–64.

144 M. A. BUFORD

examination, the ensuing items upheld as sub-scales. The brevity of such instruments, to conclude this analysis, may be sufficiently tailored for a twenty-first-century organization that is constantly competing for time.

DISCUSSION

The chief hope of this chapter was to understand if the concepts affiliated with boardroom boldness language could be developed into a scientific instrument. The findings of this study can potentially help decisions-makers do three things: (1) make better empirical choices; (2) better manage the ethical health of cultures; and (3) help decision-makers to understand the climate of followership better. Moreover, the empirical establishment of the eight sub-scales as outlined in Tables 8.24, 8.25, 8.26, 8.27, 8.28, 8.29, 8.30, and 8.31 can help to advance a reseacher's understanding of an influencer's propensity to follow unethical orders blindly or to utilize their moral imagination to stop king-think.

Table 8.24 Shut-up and comply scale

Item no	Item
SU1	It is my duty to not only comply with an unethical order but to go one step beyond it
SU2	If given the opportunity to champion an unethical order from a leader I respect, I will gladly execute it and go one step further
SU3	It is my duty to comply with an immoral order
SU4	If given the opportunity to comply with an immoral order from a leader I respect, I will execute it and do nothing more

Table 8.25 Shut-up and sabotage scale

Item no	Item
SU1	If my leader directs me to accomplish an unprincipled mission, I will secretly try to sabotage it innovatively
SU2	Unprincipled orders should be sabotaged with creative energy
SU3	It is my duty to not only disrupt an unprincipled order but to also undermine it in a unique manner
SU4	If given the opportunity to interrupt an unprincipled order from a leader I respect, I would use my best imaginative option to stop it

MEASURING YOUR ORGANIZATION'S BOARDROOM LANGUAGE   145

LIMITATIONS

This aspect of the book had several limitations. First, the study did not collect demographic data about the participants' levels of followership or their ethnic data. This ommision could have potentially skewed the data. In a similar vein, participants in the study were overwhelmingly female. A more balanced data collection could have provided a different outcome.

Table 8.26 Speak-in with a parable scale

Item no	Item
SI1	When communicating with my direct supervisor, I prefer to use stories to try to change their point of view particularly when they are wrong
SI2	When my organization is confronted with an ethical dilemma, the best course of action to help my leader to change is with an appropriate story
SI3	When a relevant historical narrative is provided to my leader, it can help them to make a moral decision
SI4	When my organization is confronted with an ethical dilemma, the best course of action to help my leader to change is to create organizational allies

Table 8.27 Speak-in on principles scale

Item no	Item
SI1	When communicating with my direct supervisor, it is important to me to stand on right principles to try to change their point of view
SI2	When my organization is confronted with an ethical dilemma, the best course of action to help my leader to change is with a values centric direct approach
SI3	If a person in the organization with a strong values-based reputation approached my leader, it can sway them to do the right thing
SI4	If my leader directs me to accomplish an unprincipled mission, approaching them privately while standing on what is right can convince them to rescind the order

Table 8.28 Speak-out negatively scale

Item no	Item
SO1	When I feel powerless in an unethical organization, I find myself using cynical conversations to make myself feel better
SO2	Unethical orders should be accomplished pessimistically
SO3	It is an acceptable organizational practice to insert negativity into the job as the team performs an unethical order
SO4	If given the opportunity to champion an unethical order from a leader I respect, I would execute it and complain to everyone along the way

146 M. A. BUFORD

Table 8.29 Speak-out nonviolently scale

Item no	Item
SO1	When I feel powerless in an unprincipled organization, I have no problem speaking out in a public and nonviolent manner
SO2	Unethical orders should be resisted with the tool of striking
SO3	It is my duty to join fellow organizational protesters to stop an unethical order or practice
SO4	If given the opportunity to execute an unethical order from a leader I respect, I would demonstrate my loyalty to the organization by protesting in a public way

Table 8.30 Step-down by resisting scale

Item no	Item
SD1	If I worked in an unethical organization, resisting flawed practices until fired is an honorable gesture
SD2	Unethical orders should be resisted even if it leads to being fired
SD3	It is my duty to resist until being fired to stop an unethical order or practice
SD4	If given the opportunity to execute an unethical order from a leader I respect, I would demonstrate my loyalty to the organization by resisting until being fired

Table 8.31 Step-down by resigning scale

Item no	Item
SD1	If I were employed by an institution that suddenly adopted an immoral policy, retirement is an appropriate tool to convey a principled message
SD2	It is my duty to send a message by retiring if I had the tenure to stop an unethical order or practice
SD3	If I were employed by an institution that suddenly adopted an immoral policy, a letter of resignation is an appropriate tool to convey a moral message
SD4	Unethical orders should be resisted by resigning

Although the Cronbach's alpha score for *step-down by resigning* was lower than the other sub-scales, at 0.79 with N = 4, the brevity of the scale may be worth the exchange. Moreover, this study could be improved by generating a larger and better quality of pool items for the *step-it-up* concept. This, coupled with the inclusion of a more purposeful demographic, could bring more empirical rigor to the study. As the construct of followership continues to develop, this section should not be viewed as an exhaustive attempt to explore the spiritual facet of leading upward, but as an initial attempt to understand and scientifically codify the phenomenon.

CHAPTER 9

The Anatomy of Bold Followership

Intelligent Disobedience

Ira Chaleff, in *Intelligent Disobedience*, makes a compelling case for training followers in how to employ the act of disobedience for organizational health. The premise of his book revolves around the training of guide dogs. People with various disabilities (i.e., seeing, diabetic) may require the assistance of "man's best friend" and the dogs are thus trained to disregard orders that would expose their master to danger. For example, if a person were blind and required the help of their guide dog to cross the street, the dog would not proceed if they heard a vehicle approaching from a distance. Though the owner may feel like it is safe to proceed, the guide would exercise "an act of peaceful noncompliance with laws or norms or the demands of authority that, if followed, would hinder the moral progress of society."[1] This small but powerful act of sitting down to save the owner's life is the essence of intelligent disobedience.

Moreover, Chaleff argues that intelligent disobedience can be summarized by the following:

[1] Chaleff, Ira. 2015. *Intelligent Disobedience*. Oakland: Berrett Koehler Publishers, Inc. [Kindle Loc. 144].

© The Author(s) 2018
M. A. Buford, *Bold Followership*, Christian Faith Perspectives in Leadership and Business, https://doi.org/10.1007/978-3-319-74530-5_9

148 M. A. BUFORD

- Understand the mission of the organization or group, the goals of the activity of which you are a part, and the values that guide you in how to achieve those goals.
- When you receive an order that does not seem appropriate to the mission, goals, or values, clarify the order as needed, then pause to further examine the problem with it, whether it involves safety, effectiveness, cultural sensitivity, legality, morality, or common decency.
- Make a conscious choice whether to comply with the order, or to resist it and offer an acceptable alternative when there is one.
- Assume personal accountability for your choice, recognizing that if you obey, you are still accountable, regardless of who issued the order.[2]

Additionally, Chaleff's book highlighted empirical work which found that "to resist destructive obedience we need to hold a stronger obedience to something else—to a value, a principle, an oath, a belief system."[3] To this end, bold followership is a model that stands firmly on the system of Judeo-Christian beliefs to protect a leader from themselves, as well as protecting the organization. This small yet powerful gesture of promptly articulating the appropriate language to those blinded by narcissism will require a prudent boldness that transcends conventional wisdom. At this point, it is fitting to briefly explore other forms of courage or boldness that a follower may be required to display as they serve their republic.

BATTLEFIELD BOLDNESS

Perhaps the most admired form of mettle in the history of humanity is that of battlefield boldness. This ability to perform a daring act of valor, above and beyond the call of duty, is the key ingredient that converts a shepherd into a king, and propels an average citizen into a celebrity. A modern-day example of this construct can be found in the life of Medal of Honor recipient Sergeant Dakota L. Meyer. Meyer's actions, as expressed in the following citation, speak for themselves:

---

[2] Ibid. [Kindle Loc. 155].
[3] Ibid. p. 77.

THE ANATOMY OF BOLD FOLLOWERSHIP   149

For conspicuous gallantry and intrepidity at the risk of his life above and beyond the call of duty while serving with Marine Embedded Training Team 2-8, Regional Corps Advisory Command 3-7, in Kunar Province, Afghanistan, on 8 September 2009. Corporal Meyer maintained security at a patrol rally point while other members of his team moved on foot with two platoons of Afghan National Army and Border Police into the village of Ganjgal for a pre-dawn meeting with village elders. Moving into the village, the patrol was ambushed by more than 50 enemy fighters firing rocket propelled grenades, mortars, and machine guns from houses and fortified positions on the slopes above. Hearing over the radio that four U.S. team members were cut off, Corporal Meyer seized the initiative. With a fellow Marine driving, Corporal Meyer took the exposed gunner's position in a gun-truck as they drove down the steeply terraced terrain in a daring attempt to disrupt the enemy attack and locate the trapped U.S. team. Disregarding intense enemy fire now concentrated on their lone vehicle, Corporal Meyer killed a number of enemy fighters with the mounted machine guns and his rifle, some at near point blank range, as he and his driver made three solo trips into the ambush area. During the first two trips, he and his driver evacuated two dozen Afghan soldiers, many of whom were wounded. When one machine gun became inoperable, he directed a return to the rally point to switch to another gun-truck for a third trip into the ambush area where his accurate fire directly supported the remaining U.S. personnel and Afghan soldiers fighting their way out of the ambush. Despite a shrapnel wound to his arm, Corporal Meyer made two more trips into the ambush area in a third gun-truck accompanied by four other Afghan vehicles to recover more wounded Afghan soldiers and search for the missing U.S. team members. Still under heavy enemy fire, he dismounted the vehicle on the fifth trip and moved on foot to locate and recover the bodies of his team members. Meyer's daring initiative and bold fighting spirit throughout the 6-hour battle significantly disrupted the enemy's attack and inspired the members of the combined force to fight on. His unwavering courage and steadfast devotion to his U.S. and Afghan comrades in the face of almost certain death reflected great credit upon himself and upheld the highest traditions of the Marine Corps and the United States Naval Service.[4]

As one reads the remarkable account of Meyer's battlefield boldness, another variable must be introduced to appreciate his actions fully. Namely, Meyer disregarded orders from higher up to sit by passively while his friends were being ambushed; this Marine *stepped it up* and turned the

---

[4]Citation. 2011. "Medal of Honor Sgt Dakota Meyer." *United States Marine Corps.* November 24. Accessed November 22, 2017.

momentum of the fight in their favor. But what was the ultimate source of Meyer's strength that equipped him to say no to flawed guidance and yes to the righteous thing? In his book, *Into the Fire: A Firsthand Account of the Most Extraordinary Battle in the Afghan War*, he explained that "as a grunt, I was resigned about death. I don't go to church. To me, organized religions seem like bureaucracies. But I believed in God. Grunts see His acts on the battlefield. Guys beside you get shot or blown up. You don't. God has a plan that we won't understand until we cross to the other side. There's no sense of obsessing about getting tagged. Either a bullet has your name on it or it doesn't. No need for philosophizing."[5] Meyer's belief in God that day put the "extra" in the "ordinary" and equipped him to serve with honor.

BOARDROOM BOLDNESS

The second form of boldness can be found in the boardroom. This entire book is dedicated to the understanding, development, and perfecting of this construct as it continues to mature. An exemplar, debatably, of the best of the boardroom languages is Colin Powell. The former Joint Chief of Staff and Secretary of State captured the essence of this construct in his book *My American Journey*. Powell says "don't be afraid to challenge the pros, even in their own backyard. Just as important, never neglect details, even to the point of being a pest. Moments of stress, confusion, and fatigue are exactly when mistakes happen. And when everyone else's mind is dulled or distracted the leader must be doubly vigilant. 'Always check small things' was becoming another of my rules."[6] This notion of not being afraid to challenge the pros, even in their own backyard is paramount and can be anchored in faith. In a similar vein as the findings of this book show, the source of Powell's conviction resided in the principles of the Lord. More specifically, Powell contends that "God provides us with guidance and inspiration."[7] It is the potency of divine insight and spiritual exhortation that can make the weak, strong, and the faint to acquire might (Ish. 40:28–31).

[5] Meyer, Dakota, and Bing West. 2012. *Into the Fire: A Firsthand Account of the Most Extraordinary Battle in the Afghan War.* New York: Random House. [Kindle Loc 3250].

[6] Powell, Colin L. 1996. *My American Journey.* New York: Random House, Inc. [Kindle Loc 1876].

[7] Ibid. [Kindle Loc 10575].

BYSTANDER BOLDNESS

A bystander's ability to intervene with the intent of mitigating a wrongful act done by a peer is the third form of boldness that needs to be explored. To properly understand this aspect of mettle, the reader's attention is once again returned to the My Lai massacre. As indicated in Chap. 3, after Charlie Company entered the village, some 500 inhabitants of My Lai were murdered at the hands of US Forces. That figure could have easily climbed if it had not been for the bystander boldness of Hugh Thompson. In *The Forgotten Hero of My Lai: The Hugh Thompson Story*, Trent Angers shines additional light on the carnage and the heroic actions of a soldier. As Hugh Thompson was flying about the area trying to identify and mark (the act of setting off colored-coded flares around a person) the wounded casualties for medical assistance, Thompson noticed the horrific actions of his fellow soldiers. While being sick to the stomach by what he witnessed, he radioed the accompanying gunship and said, "It looks to me there's an awful lot of unnecessary killing going on down there. Something ain't right about this. There's bodies everywhere. There's a ditch full of bodies that we saw. There's something wrong here."[8]

The feelings of disgust were not enough for this helicopter pilot, so Thompson took the initiative and landed his helicopter near the ditch where they observed the dead bodies. Once on ground he found Lieutenant Calley and engaged in the following confrontation:

Thompson: What's going on here, lieutenant?
Calley: This is my business.
Thompson: What is this? Who are these people?
Calley: Just following orders.
Thompson: Orders? Whose orders?
Calley: Just following...
Thompson: But, these are human beings, unarmed civilians, sir.
Calley: Look, Thompson, this is my show. I'm in charge here. It ain't your concern.
Thompson: Yeah, great job (said sarcastically).
Calley. You better get back in that chopper and mind your own business.
Thompson: You ain't heard the last of this (the pilot shouted as he made his way back to the aircraft).[9]

---

[8]Angers, Trent. 2014. *The Forgotten Hero of My Lai*. Lafayette: The Acadian House Publishing. [Kindle Loc 876].
[9]Ibid. [Kindle Loc 912].

152 M. A. BUFORD

Unfortunately, the confrontation was not enough to immediately stop the slaughter. As soon as the aircraft lifted off, Calley and his men proceeded to murder those still alive in the ditch. This act spurred Thompson to take matters into his own hands and located the surviving residents of the village before Calley. Once Thompson found them, he had them evacuated. This act of bystander boldness saved lives that day and begs the question, "What enabled Thompson to act while others passively observed?" *The Forgotten Hero of My Lai* provides a logical explanation:

> Wherever he went, whenever he spoke, Thompson was asked by reporters and admirers where he got the moral courage to stand up for what was right at My Lai. He got this question in Vietnam, in Norway, and throughout the United States. 'I tried to save the people because I wasn't taught to murder and kill,' he told one of the survivors of the massacre while in Vietnam in 1998. Clearly, his upbringing in Stone Mountain, Georgia, had a lot do with his response to the massacre. This is what predisposed him to act justly and heroically when the time came. Even as a youth, Thompson stood up to bullies who were picking on smaller, weaker boys; he learned this behavior from his father, who took on those who were condescending toward Native American Indians. Thompson's behavior was influenced also by the commitments he made as a Boy Scout – to be 'trustworthy... helpful... kind... brave... reverent.'
>
> The final and possibly most influential component of his moral and ethical fabric came from the Baptist and then the Episcopal Church. Since his youth, he had taken to heart the basic teachings of the Judeo-Christian faith tradition, including 'Thou shall do no murder' and the Second Great Commandment, 'Love thy neighbor as thyself.' One of his admirers who to him – Michael Hugo, a campus minister at Loyola Academy in Wilmette, Illinois put it this way: 'What you did... was essentially loving your neighbor in a profound way under difficult circumstances.'[10]

To state it differently and in the vernacular of this book, it was Thompson's righteousness that gave him the bystander boldness of a lion to intervene on that day.

BASIC BOLDNESS

The final form of nerve that warrants a cursory discussion is basic boldness, which is the ability of a follower to take an inward hard look and have the audacity to confront, correct, and create a healthy way forward, with

---

[10]Ibid. [Kindle Loc 2874].

THE ANATOMY OF BOLD FOLLOWERSHIP   153

Table 9.1   The biblical traits of a bold follower

Biblical traits	Scripture
Wisdom	James 1:5 – if any of you lacks wisdom, let him ask of God, who gives to all liberally and without reproach, and it will be given to him
Humility	1 Peter 5:5 – God resists the proud, but gives grace to the humble
Character	Proverbs 22:1 – A good name is to be chosen rather than great riches
Connection	Proverbs 18:16 – A person's gift makes room for them and brings them before greatness
Timing	Proverbs 15:23 – and a word spoken in due season, how good it is!
Tone	Proverbs 15:1 – a soft answer turns away wrath, but a harsh word stirs up anger
Servant's heart	Matthew 20:26 but whoever desires to become great among you, let him be your servant
Resourcefulness	Luke 16:1–8 describes a parable of a shrewd steward

God's grace. Jesus makes this point in Matthew 7:3 when He asked, "And why do you look at the speck in your brother's eye, but do not consider the plank in your own eye?[4] Or how can you say to your brother, 'Let me remove the speck from your eye'; and look, a plank *is* in your own eye?[5] Hypocrite! First remove the plank from your own eye, and then you will see clearly to remove the speck from your brother's eye." In these verses, Jesus uses the word hypocrite to condemn those who are quick to observe the blind spots in others without first taking note and removing their own. In an age that places more value on outward appearance than inner character, it takes courage to admit that one has a little fox roaming around in the vineyard of one's life. It is the bold follower that understands they can become that much more effective when dormant pain is addressed. When followers are brave enough to address their own pain and issues, their followership ability positively crystallizes, and they will see better to remove the speck from their leader's eye (Table 9.1).

THE BIBLICAL TRAITS OF BOLD FOLLOWERSHIP

Seeing better because of basic boldness can additionally help to refine a follower's temperament. The temperament, or overall disposition, of a person can make a difference in the boardroom. To this end, there seem to be eight distinct biblical traits of a bold follower that can help to bring out the best in both leader and organization.

154   M. A. BUFORD

The first trait revolves around wisdom. Wisdom takes insights gleaned from the knowledge of God's ways and applies them to the daily walk.[11] Because followers will be confronted with wicked problems, rules may not always be sufficient to help navigate the terrain. In those moments, a follower can unlock the promise of James 1:5, "If any of you lacks wisdom, let him ask of God, who gives to all liberally and without reproach, and it will be given to him." By sincerely inquiring of God in prayer, a person in a perplexing situation can receive the mind of the Lord. Such an insight will shine a light amid dark moments and allow a follower to see the way forward.

Followership humility is the second trait that can help to refine a person's boardroom language. Humility can be defined as a grateful and spontaneous awareness that life is a gift, and it is manifest as an ungrudging and unhypocritical acknowledgment of absolute dependence upon God.[12] In contrast, being proud is taking life for granted and depending on the self to manage life. When a follower decides to engage a leader in their own might and strength without the presence of God, it is destined to fail. Why? 1 Peter 5:5 indicates that "God resists the proud, But gives grace to the humble." Pride is not indigenous to leaders and it can undermine followers if they are not careful.

Proverbs 22:1 provides the third feature of a bold follower. That is, a good name is to be chosen over great riches. A good name is synonymous with having an impeccable reputation and character. This intangible variable, when missing, can distract and even cloud the act of speaking truth to power. Even if the message that the follower is presenting is truthful, it is more than likely to fall by the wayside because the messenger's name is blemished. Stated differently, the integrity of message and messenger must align. When they do, the moral volume amplifies, and it proactively removes leader, as well as organizational excuses.

The fourth trait of a bold follower entails the connections they have forged. Throughout their years of arduous labor and a commitment to excellence, an impeccable name introduced them to an array of personalities who, without hesitation, will vouch for their work ethic and name, and

---

[11] Hubbard, D. A. (1996). Wisdom. In D. R. W. Wood, I. H. Marshall, A. R. Millard, J. I. Packer, & D. J. Wiseman (Eds.), *New Bible dictionary* (3rd ed., p. 1244). Leicester, England; Downers Grove, IL: InterVarsity Press.

[12] Elwell, W. A., & Comfort, P. W. (2001). In *Tyndale Bible dictionary* (p. 618). Wheaton, IL: Tyndale House Publishers.

would gladly work with them again if given a chance. Biblically speaking, bold followers are an epitome of Proverbs 18:16, "A person's gift makes room for them and brings them before greatness." Their gift opens doors that otherwise seem locked and escorts them before people of prominence. Interestingly, these followers would never use such connections on themselves but only for the sake of others or the good of the organization.

Bold followers understand the power and leverage of timing. This fifth characteristic can not necessarily be reduced to a scientific formula, but is rather a spiritual act of discernment. Bold followers accept the fact that there is such a thing as "too late," but they also know that being "too early" can be as problematic. To illustrate the point of timing, consider the Jamaican national dish known as ackee and saltfish. Ackee, a fruit that grows like an apple, if picked too early and then eaten can result in a fatal outcome. Similarly, if one waits too late to pick it, the nutritional value that it can give is missed. As such, bold followers can discern the time and know the reality of Proverbs 15:23, "And a word spoken in due season, how good it is!"

Bold followers are often the recipients of a leader's harshness. Such ruggedness is especially magnified when king-think enters the equation. To this end, bold followers understand the importance of tone. This sixth trait of using the appropriate mannerism, vocal reflection, and the spirit of a message being delivered, is key. When a leader reacts in anger to a respectful act of intelligent disobedience, a bold follower takes counsel from Proverbs 15:1. This passage reminds an influencer that, "a soft answer turns away wrath, but a harsh word stirs up anger." It is true that the led can feed wrath back to a leader but what would that solve? It should be noted that a soft answer in the heat of the moment is a bold move that can help to cultivate a positive outcome for all parties.

Bold followers engage their leaders and organizations with a servant's heart. What is not at the forefront of the mind of these followers is themselves. On the contrary, they are constantly locating the needs of others and strive for excellence to meet it: when a co-worker is grieving, they are usually the first to call; when their leader is in the wrong, and everyone justifiably bashes them, bold followers redirect cynical conversations to positive actions; when the situation demands that they take one-mile, bold followers will go an extra mile in the name of peace. Plainly put, bold followers strive to be great by being a servant for they remember the admonishment of Jesus in Matthew 20:25–28, "You know that the rulers of the Gentiles lord it over them, and those who are great exercise authority over them.[26]

156   M. A. BUFORD

Yet it shall not be so among you; but whoever desires to become great among you, let him be your servant.[27] And whoever desires to be first among you, let him be your slave—[28] just as the Son of Man did not come to be served, but to serve, and to give His life a ransom for many."

The final trait of a bold follower is resourcefulness. This ability to find quick, ethical, and shrewd ways to resolve a tricky situation is critical. Luke 16:1–8 describes a parable of a steward who was accused of being wasteful. Considering the charge, the owner demanded an accounting of his goods. The steward did not have the means and was incapable of generating revenue through hard labor. As such, he proactively sought out the owner's debtors and resolved his affairs. This act received the praise of the owner for his resourcefulness. Verse 8 indicates that "the master commended the unjust steward because he had dealt shrewdly." To this end, the ability to act shrewdly, with limited resources, under pressure, can mitigate an array of corporate issues.

THE STRUGGLE FOR ORGANIZATIONAL HEALTH

A bold follower named Fredrick Douglas once offered some sage advice to those who wanted to incorporate change in a toxic organization. This Christian influencer gave a speech on August 3, 1857 that particularly connected with the audience when he rightfully indicated that,

> If there is no struggle there is no progress. Those who profess to favor freedom and yet deprecate agitation are [people] who want crops without plowing up the ground; they want rain without thunder and lightning. They want the ocean without the awful roar of its many waters. This struggle may be a moral one, or it may be a physical one, and it may be both moral and physical, but it must be a struggle. **Power concedes nothing without a demand. It never did, and it never will** [emphasis mine].

In the twenty-first century, if organizational health is to emerge, bold followers must demand it in a nonviolent manner.

There are two reasons why followers must demand organizational health. The first reason revolves around Colin Powell's assertion that "leaders are not gods. Their understanding is never totally clear, totally accurate, totally certain. Every leader is human… imperfectly human. Water-walkers sometimes fail, and quiet walkers sometimes end up on top."[13] To this end, the led must never assume their leaders are omniscient,

---

[13] Powell, Colin. 2012. *It Worked For Me*. New York: HarperCollins Publishers Inc. p. 98.

THE ANATOMY OF BOLD FOLLOWERSHIP   157

neither should they make them a demagogue. Leaders, even if they may not acknowledge it, become better when followers are bold. The second reason why followers must demand organizational health is because struggle has a universal price tag for progress. It is accepting the fact that toxic leaders will use negative campaigns, underhanded funding, and unethical oppositional research to maintain the status quo as well as their power.

FIVE PRACTICAL STEPS TO ENGAGE A TOXIC ORGANIZATION

Perhaps one is in a toxic organization. The question now becomes, "What steps can be practically taken to create a positive, nonviolent movement to mitigate organizational toxicity?" The following principles are offered to stimulate discussion and to challenge the reader to move from theory to practice.

1. **Cultivate basic boldness**. The supreme virtue of a person is to have the boldness to take a hard look within. This inner journey may be the most difficult to embark upon, but it can serve as the needed spark to activate bystander, boardroom, and, if need be, battlefield boldness. When a person leans upon the grace of God to confront the secret fox that has caused damage to the vineyards of life, they will find that a different level of power will rest upon their life. Such a power will make a person more relevant and more inclined to extend mercy and justice when required.

2. **Understand one's preferred boardroom language**. It can be argued that each follower has a subconscious default boardroom language that one subscribes to when king-think surfaces and the pressures are mounting. To understand one's language can better equip you to serve your respective leader and organization more effectively. For example, if a person has the propensity to speak the language of *shut up* in the face of wrong, it would be a prudent gesture to know this reality so that one can adjust accordingly. To help understand one's preferred boardroom language take the following non-scientific survey:

Personal Boardroom Language Survey

1 = Never, 2 = Rarely, 3 = Sometimes, 4 = Often, 5 = Very Often

1. I say what I mean and mean what I say.
2. I try to keep my opinions to myself and do my work.
3. I'm happy when my team wins, even if I'm not recognized.
4. I would rather get out of the way, than hinder the team.
5. I am not afraid to speak my mind in a public way.
6. I do not care what others think about me.
7. I live by the saying, be seen not heard.
8. I look for opportunities to help my leader, even if I don't like them.
9. I don't like drama and would prefer to avoid it.
10. When things are not right, I have no problem going over or around people to make it right.

Speak in	= Q1__ + Q6___	= Total___
Speak out	= Q5__ + Q10___	= Total___
Step down	= Q4__ + Q9___	= Total___
Shut up	= Q2__ + Q7___	= Total___
Step it up	= Q3__ + Q8___	= Total___

Now add up the numbers from the above scorecard. The category that registers the highest can indicate a person's preferred style of influencing in the context of the boardroom.

3. **Empirically understand the organizational climate.** Upon cultivating basic boldness and understanding one's boardroom language, an influencer can deploy the sub-scales outlined in Chap. 8, which can paint an empirical picture of the collective state of the team, and serve as a data points to drive home the following two steps.
4. **Coach for reflective leadership with the traits of a bold follower.** Because leaders are not gods, it is impossible for them to know everything. In a similar vein, it is very possible that they are also unaware of the mayhem being generated as result of their blind spot. To this end, a follower should leverage the eight traits of a bold follower to help their leader become more reflective. Reflective supervisors lead with questions, listen with empathy, learn with a level head, locate a team of rivals and leverage with empowerment. The bold follower can create the conditions for their leaders to consider being reflective behind closed doors before the fifth step is embraced.

THE ANATOMY OF BOLD FOLLOWERSHIP 159

5. **If a season of coaching for reflective leadership does not prevail, activate project bold followership in the organization.** As outlined in Chap. 7, project bold followership is a synthesis of the best of the boardroom boldness model. This nonviolent campaign is designed to either demand that senior leadership modifies their king-thinking, or to appeal to the greater consciousness of we the people to immediately act for the health of the organization.

CONCLUSION

Joab's dilemma is the quandary of the twenty-first-century workforce. Whether consciously or subconsciously, one has a propensity to default to one of the boardroom boldness languages to produce a solution. Stakeholders, customers, and those who make the bottom line strong have a moral imperative to first ask tough questions of themselves about the people, the process, and the policy. If there is an ethical misalignment and the king is wearing narcissistic clothes, then the reader must find the appropriate language, wisdom, and strength to engage. To this end, this book hopes to help the reader to get to the table and discover their voice at such a time. It may very well be a fact that everything rises and falls on leadership. However, it is also truthful, to conclude this argument, that the true success or failure of an organization rests on the shoulders of bold followership, which is an answer to the driving research question of this book.

Bibliography

Angers, Trent. 2014. *The Forgotten Hero of My Lai*. Lafayette: The Acadian House Publishing.

Ayres, B Drummond. 1971. *Army Is Shaken by Crisis In Morale and Discipline*. New York: The New York Times.

Ballman, Donna. 2012. "Why Walmart Won't Fire Striking Workers – And What That Means For You." *AOL FINANCE*. October 15. Accessed November 12, 2017. https://www.aol.com/2012/10/15/walmart-striking-workers-non-unionized/.

Barry, J. D., D. Mangum, D. Brown, M. S. Heiser, M. Custis, E. Ritzema, and D. Bomar. 2016. *Faithlife Study Bible*. Bellingham: Lexham Press.

Blair, Leonardo. 2017. "Calif. Megachurch Pastor Fred Price Jr. Steps Down Over 'Personal Misjudgments'." *Christianpost.com*. June 27. Accessed November 13, 2017. https://www.christianpost.com/news/crenshaw-christian-center-pastor-fred-price-jr-steps-down-over-personal-misjudgments-189765/.

Boschma, Janie. 2015. "When Do Americans Think They'll Actually Retire?" *The Atlantic*. June 23. Accessed November 13, 2017. https://www.theatlantic.com/business/archive/2015/06/ideal-retirement-age-work/396464/.

Bruhn, John G. 2001. *Trust and the Health of Organizations*. New York: Springer Science.

Brush, Peter. 2010. "The Hard Truth About Fragging." *HistoryNet*. July 28. Accessed October 31, 2017. www.historynet.com/the-hard-truth-about-fragging.htm/2.

Bump, Philip. 2017. "How America viewed the Watergate scandal, as it was unfolding." *The Washington Post*. 15 May. Accessed November 12, 2017.

162 BIBLIOGRAPHY

https://www.washingtonpost.com/news/politics/wp/2017/05/15/ how-america-viewed-the-watergate-scandal-as-it-was-unfolding/?utm_ term=.8c39e9820c6c.

Bunch, Lonnie. 2011. "The Washington Post." *Who's To blame for the first shot.* April 10. Accessed September 23, 2017. https://www.washingtonpost.com/ lifestyle/style/who-is-to-blame-for-first-shot/2011/04/04/AF1M5uHD_ story.html?utm_term=.19b0bc63aba7.

Camillus, John C. 2008. "Strategy as a Wicked Problem." *Harvard Business Review* May Issue.

Center, Holocaust Teacher Resource. 2017. "Adolf Hitler: A Study in Tyranny." Accessed August 5, 2017. http://www.holocaust-trc.org/the-holocaust-education-program-resource-guide/a-study-in-tyranny/.

Chaleff, Ira. 2015. *Intelligent Disobedience.* Oakland: Berrett-Koehler Publishers, Inc.

———. 1995. *The Courageous Follower.* San Francisco: Berrett-Koehler Publishers, Inc.

———. 2009. *The Courageous Follower: Standing Up To & For Our Leaders.* San Francisco, CA: Berrett-Koehler Publishers, Inc.

Chenoweth, Erica, and Maria J Stephan. 2011. *Why Civil Resistance Works: The Strategic Logic of Nonviolent Conflict.* New York: Columbia University Press.

Citation. 2011. "Medal of Honor Sgt Dakota Meyer." *United States Marine Corps.* November 24. Accessed November 22, 2017.

Cohen, Lester H. 1990. *The History of the American Revolution.* Indianapolis: Liberty Fund.

Conley, Dalton. 2003. "The Cost of Slavery." *The New York Times.* February 15. Accessed October 14, 2017. http://www.nytimes.com/2003/02/15/opinion/the-cost-of-slavery.html.

Copenhaver, Martin B. "He spoke in parables." Christian Century, July 13–20, 1994: 681.

Corrin, Amber. 2009. "Command and control must become command and feedback, says NATO commander." *Defense System.* August 19. Accessed November 24, 2017. https://defensesystems.com/articles/2009/08/19/landwarnet-mattis-command-control-c2-feedback.aspx.

Cortright, David. 2005. *Soldiers in Revolt: GI Resistance During the Vietnam War.* Michigan: Haymarket Books.

Covey, Stephen R. 2013. *The 7 Habits Of Highly Effective People: Powerful Lessons In Personal Change.* New York: RosettaBooks.

Covey, Stephen. 2006. *The Speed of Trust.* New York: FREE PRESS.

Denning, Steve. 2011. "The Four Stories You Need To Lead Deep Organizational Change." *Forbes Magazine.* July 25. Accessed October 22, 2017. https:// www.forbes.com/sites/stevedenning/2011/07/25/the-four-stories-you-need-to-lead-deep-organizational-change/#acaba1953b29.

BIBLIOGRAPHY 163

Dictionary, Collins. n.d. https://www.collinsdictionary.com/us/dictionary/english/deindividuation.

Dittmann, Melissa. 2003. "Lessons from Jonestown." *American Psychological Association*. November. Accessed October 8, 2017. www.apa.org/monitor/nov03/jonestown.aspx.

Dripchak, Valerie L., and Jamshid A. Marvasti. 2016. "Moral Injury in War Veterans: Seeking Invisible Wounds." *Social Work Today*. September/October. Accessed September 30, 2017. http://www.socialworktoday.com/archive/092116p18.shtml.

Elwell, W. A., and P. W. Comfort. 2001. *Tyndale Bible dictionary*. Wheaton IL: Tyndale House Publishers.

Engler, Mark, and Paul Engler. 2016. *This is An Uprising*. New York: Nation Books.

Farrand, Max. 1911. *The Records of the Federal Convention of 1787, Vol. I*. New Haven: Yale University Press.

Felice, William F. 2009. *How Do I Save My Honor? War, Moral Integrity, and Principled Resignation*. Lanham: Rowman & Littlefield Publishers, Inc.

Gabriel, Richard A., and Paul L. Savage. 1978. *Crisis in Command*. New York: Hill & Wang.

Gardner, R. B. 1991. *Matthew*. Scottdale, PA: Herald Press.

Gibbons-Nebb, Thomas. 2015. "Haunted by their decisions at war." *Washington Post*. March 6. Accessed September 30, 2017. https://www.washingtonpost.com/opinions/haunted-by-their-decisions-in-war/2015/03/06/db1cc404-c129-11e4-9271-610273846239_story.html?utm_term=.70391da6fc6c.

Gibney, A. 2005. *Enron: The smartest guys in the room [motion picture]*. United States: Magnolia Pictures.

Gordon, Claire. 2012. "Walmart Workers: This Is Why We're Striking And Making Black Friday Threat." *AOL Finance*. October 11. Accessed November 12, 2017.https://www.aol.com/2012/10/11/walmart-workers-this-is-why-were-striking-and-making-black-fri/.

Gorsuch, R. L. 1983. *Factor Analysis (2nd ed)*. Hillsdale, NJ: Lawrence Erlbaum Associates.

Hair, Joseph F, William C Black, Barry J Babin, and Rolph E Anderson. 2003. *Multivariate Data Analysis*. Upper Saddle River: Prentice Hall.

Haney, C, W Banks, and P Zimbardo. 1973. "A Study of Prisoners and Guards in a Simulated Prison." *Naval Research Review, 30* 4–17.

Harvey, Jerry B. 1988. *The Abilene Paradox and Other Meditations on Management*. San Francisco: Jossey-Base Publishers.

Howard, Michael, and Peter Paret. 1984. *On War*. New Jersey: Princeton University.

Hubbard, D. A. 1996. "Wisdom." In *New Bible dictionary*, by D. R. Wood, I. H. Marshall, A. R. Millard, J. I. Packer and D. J. Wiseman, 1244. Leicester, England: InterVarsity Press.

Johnson, McKinley. 2016. *The Theory of Leadership*. Lake Mary: Creation House.

164 BIBLIOGRAPHY

Kathleen D. Ryan and Daniel K. Oestreich (1998) Driving Fear out of the Workplace. Jossey-Bass. Kindle Loc 230.

Kennedy, John F. 1962. *Rice University Speech*. Rice University, Houston. September 12.

Kilduff, Marshall, and Phil Tracy. August 1, 1977. "Inside Peoples Temple." *New West* 30–38.

Kilpatrick, Carroll. 1973. "Nixon Forces Firing of Cox; Richardson, Ruckelshaus Quit." *WashingtonPost.com*. October 23. Accessed November 12, 2017. http://www.washingtonpost.com/wp-srv/national/longterm/watergate/articles/102173-2.htm.

King, Martin Luther. 1967. "Beyond Vietnam: A Time to Break Silence." Speech Delivered at Riverside Church. April 4. Accessed November 14, 2017. http://www.nytimes.com/learning/general/onthisday/big/1020.html#article.

Kneeland, Douglas E. 1973. "Nixon Discharges Cox For Defiance; Abolishes Watergate Task Force; Richardson And Ruckelshaus Out." *New York Times*. October 23. Accessed November 12, 2017. http://inside.sfuhs.org/dept/history/US_History_reader/Chapter14/MLKriverside.htm.

Kotter, John. 2009. *A Sense of Urgency*. MA: Harvard Business Press.

Larter, David B. 2017. "Lawmaker demands regular updates on combating pilot oxygen deprivation." *DefenseNews*. November 8. Accessed November 9, 2017. https://www.defensenews.com/naval/2017/11/07/lawmaker-demands-regular-updates-from-the-navy-on-combating-hypoxia/.

Leech, Nacy L, Karen C Barrett, and George A Morgan. 2008. *SPSS for Intermediate Statistics*. New York: Taylor & Francis Group.

Lindsay, Drew. 2012. "Something Dark and Bloody: What happen at My Lai?" *HistoryNet*. August 7. Accessed September 30, 2017. http://www.historynet.com/something-dark-and-bloody-what-happened-at-my-lai.htm.

Lipman-Blumen, Jean. 2005. *The Allure of Toxic Leaders*. New York: Oxford University Press.

Marker, Sandra L. 2004. *The Ritual of Riots: Discovering A Process Model U.S. Riots*. University Of Colorado: Dissertation.

Martin Luther King, Jr. 1963. *A Gift of Love: Sermons from Strength to Love and Other Preachings*. Boston: Beacon Press.

Martin, Jason. 2017. "Organizational Culture and How Enron Did it Wrong." *Linkedin*. February 23. Accessed October 7, 2017. https://www.linkedin.com/pulse/organizational-culture-how-enron-did-wrong-jason-martin-mba.

McLeod, Saul. 2007. *The Milgram Experiment*. Accessed August 27, 2017. www.simplypsychology.org/milgram.html.

McMahon, Robert J. 2003. *Major Problems in the History of the Vietnam War: Documents and Essays*. Boston: Houghton Mifflin.

McShane, Steven L., and MaryAnn Glinow. 2013. *Organizational Behavior*. New York: McGraw-Hill Irwin.

Meyer, Dakota, and Bing West. 2012. *Into the Fire: A Firsthand Account of the Most Extraordinary Battle in the Afghan War*. New York: Random House.

BIBLIOGRAPHY 165

Meyers, Sheri. 2015. "Studio 11 LA." *Why Powerful Men Cheat*. March. Accessed July 9, 2017. https://m.youtube.com/watch?v=x6oa3pz6hug.

Milgram, Standley. 1974. *Obedience to authority*. HarperCollins.

Munroe, Myles. 2002. *Understanding The Purpose And Power of Prayer*. New Kensington, PA: Whitaker House.

Murphy, Mark. 2016. "My Boss And I Have Different Communication Styles, And It's Destroying Our Relationship." *Forbes*. April 24. Accessed October 16, 2017. https://www.forbes.com/sites/markmurphy/2016/04/24/my-boss-and-i-have-different-communication-styles-and-its-destroying-our-relationship/#70fdd36e38cc.

Newman, Rick. 2010. "10 Great Companies That Lost Their Edge." *U.S. News*. August 19. Accessed October 23, 2017. https://money.usnews.com/money/blogs/flowchart/2010/08/19/10-great-companies-that-lost-their-edge.

Oppenheimer, Jerry. 2009. "The Daily Beast." *The Making of Madoff*. August 1. Accessed July 9, 2017. http://www.thedailybeast.com/the-making-of-madoff.

PBS. 2016. "The Underground Railroad." *Judgment Day part 4 PBS*. Accessed October 14, 2017. https://www.pbs.org/wgbh/aia/part4/4p2944.html.

Powell, Colin. 2012. *It Worked For Me*. New York: HarperCollins Publishers Inc.

Powell, Colin L. 1996. *My American Journey*. New York: Random House, Inc.

Press, Associated. 1995. *Civil Rights Pioneer's Book Tells Impact of Religion: History*. January 21. Accessed September 23, 2017. www.articles.latimes/1995-01-21/local/me-22523_1_civil-rights-movement.

Pruthi, Sandhya. 1998. "Narcissistic personality disorder." *Mayo Clinic*. Accessed August 5, 2017. http://www.mayoclinic.org/diseases-conditions/narcissistic-personality-disorder/basics/symptoms/con-20025568.

Pugh, Derek S, and David J Hickson. 2000. *Great Writers on Organizations*. Burlington: Ashgate Publishing Limited.

Raubenheimer, J. E. 2004. "An item selection procedure to maximize scale reliability and validity." *South African Journal of Industrial Psychology, Vol 30 No 4* 59–64.

Reilly, Robyn. 2014. "Five Ways to Improve Employee Engagement Now." *GALLUP News*. January 7. Accessed November 1, 2017. http://news.gallup.com/businessjournal/166667/five-ways-improve-employee-engagement.aspx.

Rosenberg, Jennifer. 2017. "The Jonestown Massacre." *ThoughtCo*. August 3. Accessed October 8, 2017. https://www.thoughtco.com/the-jonestown-massacre-1779385.

Ross, Brain. 2002. "Enron Destroyed Documents by the Truckload." *ABC News*. January 29. Accessed October 9, 2017. abcnews.go.com/WNT/story?id=130518&page=1.

Schaufeli, W. B., M Salanova, V. Gonzales-Roma, and A. B. Bakker. 2001. "The measurement of engagement and burnout: A two sample confirmatory factor analytic approach." *Journal of Happiness Studies* 3, 71–92.

166   BIBLIOGRAPHY

Schneider, Tim. 2012. "Leadership Insight: Skin in the game; are you interested or invested." *Evancarmichael.* Accessed November 1, 2017. http://www.evancarmichael.com/library/tim-schneider/Leadership-insight--Skin-in-the-Game-Are-You-Interested-or-Invested.html.

Sehgal, Kabir. 2016. "How to Write Email with Military Precision." *Harvard Business Review.* November 22. Accessed October 21, 2017. https://hbr.org/2016/11/how-to-write-email-with-military-precision.

Severance, Paul Michael. 2005. *Characterizing the Construct of Organizational Unity of Effort In the Interagency National Security Policy Process.* Falls Virginia: Proquest Doctoral Dissertation.

Spilerman, Seymour. 1970. "The causes of Radical Disturbances: A Comparison of Alternative Explanations." *American Sociological Review 36.3,* 627–649.

Streep, Peg, and Alan Bernstein. 2014. *Quitting.* Philadelphia, PA: Da Capo Press.

Thompson, James C. 2010. *The Dubious Achievement of the First Continental Congress.* Alexandria, VA: Commonwealth Books.

Tomlinson, Lucas. 2017. "Navy instructor pilots refusing to fly over safety concerns; Pence's son affected." *Fox News Politics.* April 4. Accessed November 9, 2017. http://www.foxnews.com/politics/2017/04/04/navy-instructor-pilots-refusing-to-fly-over-safety-concerns-pences-son-affected.html.

Walsh, Chris. 2014. *Cowardice: A Brief History.* Princeton, NJ: Princeton University Press.

Washington, George. 1783. "George Washington Speech." *Maryland Archives.* December 23. Accessed November 13, 2017. https://www.google.com/search?source=hp&ei=hT8JWsL-LMHSmwGZy4ugAg&q=george+washington+resignation+speech&oq=George+Washington+res&gs_l=psy-ab.1.3.0l10.2723.12701.0.16959.25.23.2.0.0.0.106.1923.19j3.22.0....0...1.1.64.psy-ab..1.24.1973...46j0i131k1j0i10k1j.

———. 1775. "The Papers of George Washington digital edition." *General Orders.* July 7. Accessed September 24, 2017. http://rotunda.upress.virginia.edu/founders/GEWN-03-01-02-0040.

Weick, Karl. 1979. *The Social Psychology of Organizing.* New York: McGraw-Hill.

Williams, Ray. 2011. "Why we choke under pressure and what to do about it." *Psychology Today.* June 24. Accessed September 24, 2017. https://www.psychologytoday.com/blog/wired-success/201107/why-we-choke-under-pressure-and-what-do-about-it.

Winston, Bruce. 2002. *Be a Leader for God's Sake.* Virginia Beach, VA: Regent University-School of Leadership Studies.

Yulk, Gary. 2010. *Leadership in Organizations.* New Jersey: Prentice Hall.

Zak, Paul J. 2017. *Trust Factor.* New York: AMACOM.

Zimbardo, Philip G. 2007. *The Lucifer Effect: Understanding How Good People Turn Evil.* New York: Random House.

Zimbardo, Phillip. 2008. "The psychology of evil." *Ted Talks.* February. Accessed August 28, 2017. https://m.youtube.com/watch?v=OsFEV35tWsg.

INDEX

A
Accountability, 15, 24, 29–30, 78, 148
Analytical communicator, 60

B
Basic boldness, 152–153, 157, 158
Battlefield boldness, 148–150, 157
Biblical prayer, 12
Boardroom boldness, xiii, xiv, 18, 41,
 57–58, 70–72, 88–89, 104–105,
 107, 114, 116–117, 119–124,
 144, 150, 159
Bystander boldness, 151–152

C
Championing the order, 47–50
Choke factor, 30–31
Communicator, 60, 65, 115
Comply with an order, 50–52, 54, 56,
 121, 131, 144, 148
Creatively sabotage the order, 54–57

E
Ethical pause, the, 45–47, 50, 58

F
Fierce urgency of now, the,
 110, 113

G
Godly inner circle, 15

H
Historical trust, 69–70

I
Illusion of taking charge, the, 32
Inspiration, 16, 32, 33, 149, 150
Intelligent disobedience,
 147–148, 155
Intuitive communicator, 60

© The Author(s) 2018
M. A. Buford, *Bold Followership*, Christian Faith Perspectives in Leadership
and Business, https://doi.org/10.1007/978-3-319-74530-5

167

168 INDEX

K
King-think, 17–19, 46, 56, 61,
65, 71, 79, 91, 92, 97, 99,
113, 114, 119, 144, 155,
157, 159

L
Little foxes, 3–4, 10, 13, 15, 18, 115
Logos therapy, 10–12, 14
Lust of the eyes, 3–6, 11
Lust of the flesh, 3, 4, 6–8, 11, 13

M
Moral loyalty, 30

N
Narcissism, 8, 18, 119, 148

O
Operational righteousness, 35
Organizational diseases, xiv, 73–89, 119

P
Parable, 60–65, 72, 114, 134, 135,
145, 153, 156
Personal communicator, 60, 65
Prayerful 1st step, 26
Pride of life, 3, 8–11, 18
Principled resignation, 100
Proactivity, xiii, 32, 46, 59, 62,
112–114, 120, 124, 125, 127,
143, 154, 156

R
Resist until fired, 97–99, 141
Retire, 77, 100, 103, 123, 141, 146
Righteous, 34–39, 41, 56, 60, 70, 82,
83, 85, 102, 115, 150, 152

S
Self-awareness, 11–12
Shut up, 43, 47, 48, 54, 58, 114,
115, 125, 128–132, 137, 144,
157, 158
Signs and wonders, 88
Silent moral, 46–47
Speak in, 59, 60, 62, 66, 68, 71, 89,
114, 115, 119, 125, 132–135,
137, 145, 158
Speaking in with principles,
68–69, 72
Speaking in with strategic pack, 65–68
Speaking out by whining, 81
Speaking out by whistle-blowing, 86
Speaking out with a whisper,
83–86, 114
Speak out, 83, 84, 114, 115, 125,
127, 135–138, 145, 146, 158
Spirituality, 26, 47, 70
Step down, xiv, 96, 100–102, 104, 114,
116, 125, 139–143, 146, 158
Step in up, 20, 131, 143
Straight talk, 70
Strategic righteousness, 37

T
Tactical righteousness, 35
Transparency, 28, 29

CPSIA information can be obtained
at www.ICGtesting.com
Printed in the USA
LVOW13*0858110518

576724LV00013B/250/P